TALES OF MY SKIN

BIODUN ABUDU

Lalibra Books
Antioch, CA 94509
http://www.lalibrabooks.com

Printed in the United States of America
First Edition, 2011

Cover Illustration by: Anna Wilkenfeld

ISBN-10: 0615548970
ISBN-13: 978-0615548975

LALIBRA BOOKS

TALES OF MY SKIN

IS

BASED ON A TRUE LIFE STORY

DEDICATION

My Open Letter to the Unknown

Biodun means born in celebration and my destiny in life has never been to be locked in the corner of a room. What I do, what I wear, who I am, my decisions, what I write, how I walk and act all together brings happiness to my soul. Gone are the days when I had no one to wipe my tears as I suffered daily. Thank God my thoughts of suicide are now a thing of the past. I was born to make history.

I will forever remain a mystery that is unsolvable and I will still remain undefined, uncategorized and most of all unpredictable. Forever will I be a lover of all humans because God is Love and if you have the boldness to point out to someone in disgust or hate then you don't love God. *1 John 4:20 If anyone says, "I love God," yet hates his brother, he is a liar. For anyone who does not love his brother, whom he has seen, cannot love God, whom he has not seen.*

I have chosen my path to be the voice for my peers who are scared to say that I have been raped of my worth but that does not define me. I do not want to fight for rights that we or I deserve but I want to handle what is here and present to make it my home and not a battlefield. Spreading love on earth is human nature and only God can judge

Thanks Biodun

PREFACE

Everyday people walk past teenagers and even younger children of varying ages and don't stop to think what stories may lay behind their youthful eyes. When you walk past these young individuals you would never stop to think which of them may have been raped, mistreated, or sexually abused by male and more frequently these days' even female family members. Let alone whether some obtrusive act was committed upon them by a next door neighbor or frequent babysitter that the family may have come to trust. Through these experiences children without knowing begin to mimic what their parents, siblings and other adults do as part of what they consider their daily routine.

That porn which was accidentally left in the DVD player which a child may have come upon or the adult magazine that Dad left laying around all further serve to influence the sexual growth of a child.

At the age of 10 and younger, some boys have already had at least their first girlfriend, may have had their first same sex relationship or experience, or in very severe cases have experienced an intimacy with an adult. In my country Nigeria, there are cases where by the age of thirteen a young girl may have already taken on a husband who is forty years her senior.

In Nigeria it is common for a child to be forced into the pornography industry, prostitution or any other numerous horrors due to desperation from their existing circumstances. There are instances where you hear of a child who may have been forced by an adult to sleep with an animal for the adult's pleasure or satisfaction. Going through these horrors, it is no surprise that for a child at the age of fifteen it is difficult to know what real love is or can be with someone who has no agenda but to love you. . I myself have been in several of these situations and know of several others who have experienced it directly. The key to surviving these horrendous times in our lives was to smile, socialize as though nothing was going on, continue with our studies as we were expected to and more importantly remain silent. This is where my story begins.

1

This is where my silence ends. Even now I am still waiting for the right moment, that safe moment to give myself permission to release and free that sad part of me. I have chosen to deal with my experiences during my childhood a bit differently than most.

To properly introduce myself, my name is BabaTunde Adeniyi. I was born in New York, here in the United States but raised in Lagos Nigeria. Most people I came into contact with here in the US when I was younger would describe me as a Black American kid with an African background. In Nigeria everyone knew me as Tee, sometimes as Ayo (when I would instruct them), but here, they always knew me as the African kid whose name they could never pronounce. More formally most knew me as Tunde Williams.

To be clear, most of the formal moments only came when I would introduce myself after rolling over from a night of sex with someone who I barely knew. I am 5'11, weigh about 165lbs, have an athletic build and am rather handsome, some would say even cute facially. Although in truth, it's been mostly my rear end that has received the most attention and conversation from men and always in relation to some bedroom activity. I've definitely had my share of wild times but it's the life that I created online that was the one that got me out and emotionally stripped from head to toe.

When I was a boy, my parents trained me as best as they could and taught me about life and the many pitfalls I might encounter. I heard about abstaining from the dangers of the world but I didn't want to abstain, I wanted to dip full body into the real world and experience it firsthand. The old saying goes, "a word to the wise" but for me I have always believed that it's not until a person falls flat on his face that he realizes his mistakes'. That's the only true time a person can begin to pick themselves back up and begin to listen and heed what people have told them all along would happen is after they have fallen head first into the muck. For a long time I thought that I could live my life without ever dealing with or acknowledging the nightmares that would haunt me from my childhood. What I discovered in the end was that was the furthest thing from the truth.

Whenever I would get into a new relationship or even meet a potential new love interest, two of the get to know questions that I would always be asked was, "What age did you first have sex?" or "Who was the first person you had sex with?" I would always hesitate before answering, not because I wasn't brave enough to answer or that I was fearful, the main reason I would hesitate, was that I felt it was never the right moment to answer as truthfully as I wanted.

2

Growing up my whole family had always seen me as the boy who was sweet, innocent and handsome and always wanted to be different. Most of all I was the child who, one way or the other was extremely strong willed. They were right in that perception of me, but what they didn't know was that I also was the young boy with many deep secrets and pain that most would only attribute to a life associated with an adult. While other children my age were busy expanding their vocabularies, the only words I knew quite well were those that had to do with or involved sex. But I did not dare tell a soul about any of what was going on; instead I continued to suffer in silence.

I come from a family of two other siblings, one sister and one brother. Even though later on in life, I would hear of my Dad having fathered several children.

To this day I haven't been able to confirm or deny their existence. I am eldest of my siblings and everyone has always told me that I needed to be the one to pave the way for the others.

Our extended family is rather large, I have lots of uncles, aunts and so many cousins that I couldn't even begin to list them, most of who are females, which had a great influence on my life as a young man. My cousins took me everywhere with them so it was natural that I picked up their mannerisms along the way. Early on, I can remember having believed that I was a woman myself because I couldn't understand why I was in the midst of all these women without having been one myself. I often told myself that I didn't have breast, hair or features like a woman because I was just simply a different kind of woman.

When I was six my mom left me with my Dad and his new wife in the US so she could return to Nigeria to open up a business. I hated living with my Dad; it was a nightmare from the first day.

I remember sleeping on a small cot in the corner of his bedroom where he and his wife slept in their small New York apartment. I remember dreading when night time would come, because there would be one of two things on the TV that my dad would always watch.

It would either be *Tales of the Crypt*, which would scare me so badly I would lay there awake for most of the night. Or he would be watching a pornographic movie for him and his wife. I would have to lay there on that cot and listen to them having sex. I would have to pretend like I was sleeping because they would rush me off to bed when they wanted their alone time, but sometimes it was hard getting to sleep and I would be laying there, wishing for them to finish.

It was about this time that I started wetting the bed. The first few times I did it my Dad would give me a spanking. So I started conditioning myself to get up earlier so I could clean up any evidence that I had wet my bed.

When my Dad would have to travel for work, my stepmother used these opportunities to take her frustrations and hatred of my mother out on me. I remember occasions where she would cook and eat and not give me any. Or if I complained enough about not having any food, she would cook, eat and then whatever was left back on her plate I was allowed to eat. I would have to sneak into the kitchen and steal little boxes of cereal when she was asleep when I got really hungry. Whenever I told my Dad what had happened while he was gone, it would fall on deaf ears, so after awhile I simply didn't say anything.

My mom sent for me when I was around eight or nine after she had began her business and gotten somewhat settled. After I left the US to return to Nigeria, I never heard from my Dad again. I sometimes wondered if he even thought about whether I was alive or dead. It's not as though when I was finally able to start living with my mom again in Lagos when I was around nine that things were any better. We moved around a lot, and I sometimes felt as though I never had a constant place to stay other than school. When we stayed with other family or friends I would have random nannies who always seemed to be older males to care for me. I am not sure what caused it all to start; maybe it was because even when I was younger I had feminine characteristics, but they always seemed to have an opportunity take full advantage of me.

Back then, I saw it as love that men gave people who they wanted to be with but in reality it couldn't have been further from anything than love, it marked the beginning of my years of abuse. On one such occasion, I remember staying with our neighbors while my mother had gone to work. They had a son who was several years older than me, I am not sure why this particular instance stood out more for me, perhaps it's because it came from someone who was also young like me, I never knew I had to distrust other children as well.

I was crying because my mother had just dropped me off and I wanted to be at home. "Why are you crying?" he asked. "Your mom will be back soon."

"She always says she will be back and I never see her until its night time," I answered still sobbing.

"She loves you though you know that right?" he asked looking at me to answer.

"I don't know if she does love me, I think she loves her friends more."

"What friends?"

"Plenty of friends, some who are boys and even your daddy, is one of her friends."

"Oh, those kind of friends, we can be those kind of friends too," he said. By this time I was confused about what he was talking about.

"But in order for us to be friends you must do something for me first," he said.

"What do I have to do?" I remember asking.

He never really said anything after that, he simply grabbed me and placed his lips on mine. I remember not really being alarmed; I just thought it was a way that friends could show each other affection. I can remember kissing him back and being happy that I had a friend that cared so much about me.

I called him my best friend and wanted to always go over to his house because he would give me things and be nice to him if I complied with all the ways he came up with to show his love for me.

As a kid I was somewhat of a day dreamer. I would imagine that I was on stage dancing and singing for people as an entertainer. Whenever my mother wasn't around I would grab her heels and wig and dance to the latest Janet Jackson music video that played on the TV.

By the time I had gotten to high school all I could think about was performing. One of my teachers told me that dancing was simply another kind of art and that I should continue to do it if that was my dream. After that I began participating in plays at my school sometimes even being female characters where I would have to dress in drag.

I can't recall every having any sexual experience with girls. There was one girl that I had a crush on and to this day I am not sure what exactly attracted me to her, but I do remember being sad when she came and told me her family was moving. Her name was Morenike Adisa and that day when she came and told me I remember having begged her for a kiss goodbye. She did allow me to kiss her but that was as far as it went. And after she left, I returned to being my usual self, and being even more feminine than I was before I had met her.

3

People who I meet in the community today always want to know what the African gay scene was like and I always tell them how it was according to how gay life was for me. For me, back then it was about me most of the time. I always wanted to be myself in most ways and I loved being open, showing off my legs, wearing tight jeans, wearing tight school uniforms which I always accentuated by unbuttoning my school uniform shirt to show off what I thought of as my man cleavage. By the time I was fifteen, there were definitely admiring eyes both female and male, especially males in my school and even some of the male teachers. Everyone in my school knew who I was, many said I was gay, some said I only acted like that because I had so many sisters and few brothers to show me what they felt it meant of what it was to be a man.

For me that wasn't the case, I only always told people that I had five sisters because I wanted to skip the questions when they asked me why I walked a certain way or how it was that I danced so much better than the girls or even why all my mannerisms and thinking was more feminine that masculine. I didn't' care about any of that, all the while I was thinking that all it was that I really wanted was for one male to love me for the rest of my life. Eventually I did find someone to do just that, love me.

But in terms of knowing how to function as a gay man, I didn't learn any of that until I came to the US. I didn't know anything preparing myself for sex. It was my friend Bryan who explained to me about taking an enema before I knew I was going to have sex or douching before I had sex to make sure there were no accidents during sex. Before that, I just took it to be one of the things you had to deal with when you had anal sex. Because while I was not necessarily sexually experienced when I was younger neither were the guys I was dealing with so we were both naïve to the routine that needed to occur.

4

My first official boyfriend was Nonso Fadeyi. I first laid eyes on him when he was introduced as the new kid in my school. As was typical, whenever the teacher would introduce someone new in the class all the kids would flock to him or her after class to get to know them or be friends with him. I had an immediate physical attraction to him when I saw him, but instead of flocking to him after class like the other kids, I did the total opposite. I completely ignored him like many school girls do when they are interested in a boy. It was just my luck that first day, when the school bus arrived to take us to our respective homes; he also ended up on the same bus as me.

Throughout that first bus ride I continuously stared at him and each time he would look glance around and back in my general direction; I would turn my head quickly and look in the other direction. Watching him even in those furtive moments made me happy that he had at least looked in my direction but I was even happier when I found out that he was the new neighbor that had moved in a few days before behind our apartment.

Nonso lived with his mom, dad, brother and sister right behind in an apartment that was about the same size as ours. His father was a pastor and he had invited my family over for prayer meetings and to their church services on a couple of occasions. Every time we attended and there would be a closing prayer I always made sure I ended up right beside him because then I would get to at least hold hands with him.

Since we were in the same class, lived in the same compound complex and attended church services together, it was only natural that we became close in general. We waited for the bus in the morning and we waited for it after classes, so it was a regular event for us. And whenever I was sick and hadn't come to school he would come knocking my door after school to check on me and update me about what had happened in class. As each day passed by we both got to know about each other families. He and I both were the eldest of our siblings and he like I was in charge of raising his brother and sister. Except Nonso was more of a disciplinarian in his family that I in mine.

One day he had come over to check on me and I happened to be at our apartment by myself which was rare. He had come by to check up on me and see if I wanted to hang out. It was the first time he had come over when I hadn't missed a class so I was excited about the visit. We were sitting in my room on the bed talking about one of the upcoming projects in our class when suddenly the look on his face changes as we were talking. All of a sudden he smiled and poked me in my tummy right above the navel. It was such an awkward and unexpected gesture that my only response was to jump on him and the next thing I knew we were wrestling around on my bed, but playfully.

I noticed while we were wrestling his manhood had become erect and had caused his shorts to totem. And right then I knew that he was attracted to me. I am still not sure what caused me to be so bold, but I took advantage of the opportunity and I grabbed his manhood. I remember being a little scared because I didn't know what he was going to do, whether he was going to slap me or beat me up. He did neither; instead he started to kiss me in return. We had sex right then and there in my living room on the coffee table. That moment has always remained unforgettable and since that time we grew stronger together. Even his brother and sister noticed a change in him as he hardly disciplined them anymore because he was so preoccupied spending his time with me.

The only time I ever recall him getting upset with me was the one time one of the kids at school started a rumor about me having a crush on one of the girls in our class. When Nonso found out about it he ignored me all day at school even though I remembered telling him it wasn't true. He even managed to corner me in our compound regarding the issue.

"Just open the door," I remember him saying to me when I came to the front door. As I opened it he brushed past me with such force I would have lost my balance had I not stepped back to brace myself.

"So is it true what they are saying?" he asked through clenched teeth.

"No, I don't like her like that," I said. "She's just my friend."

I could see from the look in his eyes that nothing I said was going to matter. I didn't even see the slap coming as it landed on my face. I was so stunned about his reaction the slap that I didn't bother to get out of the way as he reached for me, grabbing me in a bear hold. He proceeded to remove his best and beat me. I couldn't, maybe I didn't want to fight back because I did love him and I didn't want to defend myself and hurt him in the process. So I laid there and took it, thinking in some way I deserved it even though I had done nothing wrong. As he was beating me, he was explaining why he was beating me.

"I love you and I don't want anyone to take you from me," he was saying between the swings of his belt. All I could do was lay there balled up and crying. I was too weak at this point to fight back.

When it was over, he simply said in a raspy heavy breathed tone, "I'm sorry I didn't mean to beat you, I was just angry."

"Leave me alone," was all I could muster in return. Then he started to cry as he sat there next to me still curled up on a ball on the floor. He lay there next to me, kissing my face and neck. I was so overwhelmed with what had just happened that I didn't stop him from kissing me, I laid there and let him make love to me on the floor still sore from the beating. The one thing I didn't want was for him to leave me, it was my biggest fear of getting close to someone that they would ultimately leave.

With Nonso I experienced a love that was deep and at times painful. It was nerve racking coming up with reasons to my mother as to why I had bruises every now and again. I so was scared of being alone that I settled for the treatment from him. After all, I was watching my mother going through the same thing with her boyfriend at the time. So to a degree it was normal, it was expected.

My mother never left him and they always fought so it made sense that it was ok every now and again that I needed to be disciplined as well. Eventually we moved from that compound to another location which was not close enough for me to make visits to see Nonso. Once again I was back with that lonely feeling of having no one to love or to love me.

5

When I was dating Nonso I was able to finally start at least experiencing something in life, fun, fear, challenges and drama. While I was dating him, I would get propositioned by straight men or at least those who emphatically proclaimed to be, married men who had kids my age and I would without his knowledge, entertain their requests willingly. I didn't know what it meant to control my sexual urges or where those urges were stemming from when they would come on.

Nonso and I had a similar story to one another, and it was evident because our sexual appetites required us to engage in sex multiple times a day. Except I wasn't just having sex with him, even though I would have never admitted that to him   Looking back, we were not all about sex because we enjoyed going out together and experiencing the world. Everyone we would meet in Nigeria presumed we were simply best friends and we kept it that way, it made life easier. It wasn't until we fought that our school and sometimes our families would know that there was something more intimate going on between us.

Our relationship was so predictable; he would spend all his money on me buying candy, clothes and delivering many 'I am sorry' letters, always leaving them at my house or on my desk at school. No matter how much I would think I hated him when he would beat me I always remembered he was there for me and he was more than my lover at that time he was the missing male figure I didn't have growing up which I so desperately needed.

Sometimes when we would be experience one of our youthful relationship crises I would end up crying in my room and I wouldn't eat for days. My mom always thought it was because of something she might have done to make me angry. But it never was, and I couldn't explain what it was instead about a beating I had experienced with my boyfriend.

In Nigeria, I never knew the terms bottom, top, versatile, versatile bottom, versatile top, masculine, feminine or any of the other myriad of terms to describe gay men. I was just living life the best way I knew how. The few gay people I did know about were living in secret and that was as far as it went in terms of a community. The only time people in the community found out someone was gay was if they were caught in the act of having sex with someone. Sometimes I wanted to be able to say to them, "I am just like you." Young boys who were caught having sex were publically outed or embarrassed during school assemblies. Some were expelled totally dependent on how "severe" their cases were taught to be.

Nonso and I never actually sat down to discuss what we were doing together. We never called it anything except love. We knew in Nigerian society it was wrong so we never displayed it in public but other than that we would sometimes sit down and talk about our hopeful future of living together and running away to enjoy our freedom. I knew he dated and liked girls before he met me and I was the first boy he had ever been attracted to he had told me one time. I don't think at our level we knew the word "bisexual" for someone like himself but the word "gay" was known.

I remember he would sometimes say to me, "It would have been perfect if you were born a girl."

6

In 2007 I really began getting involved with the gay culture and I was excited and curious about the new found gay freedom I have in the United States. For me the internet was an easy more convenient way of finding out about the gay lifestyle. I will never forget, on Feb 21st 2007 I made my first foray by simply inputting the word 'Gay' into the search engine. Little did I know I was going to be given more than what I thought I was asking for when I typed those three letters onto the screen. The results that were returned to me included everything from informative articles, websites, social sites and porn. As I began navigating my way through I noticed more things about the gay culture I hadn't known before through the websites and more so through the porn sites. I began venturing into the chat rooms and began conversing with a few people about their lives and about being gay.

It was surprising to see how they would let in on all the stories and experiences that they may have had in the community, but somehow that wasn't enough for me. Merely chatting became insufficient for my desire, so I decided to take a chance and meet some of the men in person in hopes that maybe I would be able to find my next lover through the misted portals of the internet. My search began feeling as though I were interviewing or applying for a job when I would complete my online searches. I sought out places where men hung in Chicago to meet other men.

One of the places I first visited was calling Boys Village. I remember before I even visited for the first time, I walked by a few times to scope it out and see how it was in there. It was located in the northern part of Chicago along a strip that was filled with other clubs, bars, restaurants, and stores which specifically catered to the gay and lesbian community. There were a few straight people I could tell that came through this area of town as well. It was a moment of pure freedom to be able look at a guy without feeling guilty or embarrassed and I felt as though I was in paradise, finally.

It was at this time that I began to have my real American experience in the gay community. I began seeing men who identified as gay, bisexual or some who still called themselves straight. There were so many men that I began to compare them to animals and I would picture them belonging to a specific species of animal. I would classify the way they functioned, thought, behaved, and reacted to certain situations.

I called my research the 13 types of gay men which a great online friend of mine had provided me:

1. The Peacock
Good looking and full of pride. Highly egoistic and often perceived to be emotional less because of the non descriptive facial expressions they wear all the time. They tend to have very high morals and they believe in giving just enough space for extracurricular play to their partners and expect utmost honesty in return. They have complete faith in you and believe in everything you say, try to fool around and you are nailed.

2. The Hyena
Always ready for some fun and laughter but all the while ready to ultimately at the end of the night get their prey. They are smooth talkers; you'll often see them exchanging phone numbers with good looking guys in office corridors and even before you wake up with the next morning they have already arranged another rendezvous with their new prey. These guys believe in the motto of "any one will do". They have a much larger sexual repertoire than their other colleagues in the gay animal kingdom. They are highly promiscuous and can and will sleep with anyone.

3. The Antelope
They are one of the cutest and most selfless beings you'll see around. They are honest and firm believers of their particular set of values. They are most often timid, intelligent, polite and generally monogamous when in a relationship. They love to get

indulged in luxuries. They appreciate articulate, sophisticated and chivalrous men. Once they are in love with you then all your worries become theirs.

4. The Guinea Pig
Bless you if you are seeing or in a relationship with a guinea pig. These types of guys often fall under the 'mama's boy' category. They will listen to her and only her and your monster-in-law mother will not allow him get close to you. These guys are fickle and spineless. They may love you but will never say so for fear of their family's reaction. However they do expect everyone around them to love them and show it as well, which is because of the insecurity they inherently suffer.

5. The Platypus
It's not hard to find platypus in your midst. This species is most widely available and can be found at any of the gay social spots. They are often loud mouthed, psychoanalytical and besides their appearance (which isn't pleasing either) they love to criticize anything and everything. Their wardrobe typically consists of garish colors and they are typically clothed in pink t-shirts and golden shoes. Ask them a simply question like "What is a mimosa?" and they can most certainly write a book about it. They think to the world of themselves and are always involved in name dropping.

6. The Orangutan
Beware of the orangutan because it just might be your best friend. These types of guys were often commitment types who loved mischief too much; they were once obedient towards their partner and pokerfaced. 'Well read, well bread' suits them and they are not shy to 'experiment if requested. You'd never know when they did what they did and they know to keep their secrets well. Don't be amazed if they have slept with your boyfriend and still manage to hangout around you as if nothing ever happened.

7. The Horse

Enthusiastic and raring to go for new opportunities they will easily leave you for someone better looking at anytime. You cannot afford to look like less than if you are in a relationship with them. If you have a horse living with you, then you better be careful and keep your eyes open. My best advice is to start taking care of you and join a yoga class, gym or anything else that you can to maintain your weight and figure.

8. The Dog

This species is on the verge of extinction, and are the most desired in the community. They are committed, monogamous, and humble and won't shy away from long term relationships. They have a good taste in the arts and literature. You can always get PDA without requesting it so just enjoy it. You are lucky if you have and can keep a dog. Just a word of caution, they will and do expect the same treatment in return from you.

9. The Snail

Snails are slow, steady, old fashioned, like to take their time before they commit to you and at the same time they are the biggest emotional fools. They always end up getting hurt in the bargain. They do however know how to be happy alone. Snails are good painters, cooks and enjoy career fields such as yoga instructor or meditation facilitator. They ultimately just want you to take care of them.

10. The Wolf

Wolves are lonesome, yet happy, always looking for that someone special. But in their endless search they don't realize that they have missed many beautiful chances. These guys are perfectionists and enjoy spending quality time at very exotic, faraway places. It's very easy to be over looked by a wolf. You need to know how to make that lasting impression which will keep them glued to you. Just as an advice, be yourself when you are around them, it works every time.

11. The Snake
Snakes are protectors. Remember seeing those under nourished, skimpy clad women at the pubs with 'hulks' around them, those guys are absolute snakes. They will be by your side come whatever may, venomous for others who try to explore their territory (you). Get use to possessiveness. These types are wild in bed, so have fun and enjoy.

12. The Koala
These creatures are too stuck in their splendiferous yesteryears. It's foolish to expect them to venture out of their mental green and fruitful glorious past. This doesn't mean they don't want you, they do but however much ever you try; you'll always be compared with their ex.

13. The Parasite
This guy is none other than our friendly leech like individual who will live off of you. They suck you financially, emotionally, mentally, sexually and if possible in any other manner. They just want to live off someone and if it someone who can love them as well then that's a plus. These guys are habituated to getting everything in life that is easy.

I have at some point and time encountered each of these types. I can say that each time, it helped to sharpen my awareness and protect my surroundings. In my world I sampled many candies in the community, different flavors all so tasty in their own way. Some hurt your tummy after indulging, some left me wanting more and some left me having unwanted and needless cavities.

7

I found myself looking for love in all the wrong places every time and in all the faces of all kinds of men. I even managed to pull well respected men famous men in their 30's who I shall not mention by name, who maintained wives and kids all throughout our relationship. I had no sense of direction and I thought that sex would make a man stay with me or at least fall in love with me. In living this cycle and culture I failed to understand the true meaning of no strings attached sex. I always felt that if a person like me was online looking for love or could go to a club then I might be lucky enough to find someone else like myself searching for the same thing.

I began to get so engrossed in searching different websites that it used up my hours of sleep, energy and eventually even my dignity. There were three websites that seemed to catch my attention the most. They were called <u>Adam 4 Steve</u>, <u>Black Gay Conversation</u> and <u>Carmenslist</u>.

First came Carmenslist, it was a website that had various sections and classified fields. The different sections covered a wide range of topics, including jobs, forums, housing etc. However, it was the personals section that I began my foray. I would head straight into the men seeking men option and on occasion I would go under the men for women just to be curious as to what people were seeking in that section. I would read through the posts, only certain ones would capture my attention enough for me to click on the actual ad for me to read about exactly what the person was looking for in a date. I noticed one commonality in the ads that I answered, that people had problems when it came to being straight and to the point. For example if I would request a photo, they would not send a picture back after having received mine, or they would rudely not respond for whatever reason. So I ultimately ended up making it easy on myself by going ahead and posting in an ad of my own. My ad read:

> *I am tired of the never ending email exchanges that end up leading all the way to...NOTHING? So if you are interested and you're ready to take the 4-email challenge, I look forward to hearing from you.*
>
> > *Email #1 = you reply with your accurate age, stats, approximate location and what you're into. Include a photo.*

Email #2 = I reply to your email -- EVEN IF I'M NOT INTERESTED -- with my photo, because it's only fair!
Email #3 = If email #2 indicates interest on my part, you view the photo that I've sent, and tell me yes or no. If it's a yes...
Email #4 = I send my cell # and we're ready to meet up.

After posting my ad I didn't have to wait very long before someone replied to me with an email title which read **'Wife out of town looking to have fun with a guy tonight'.** I was so desperate to meet up with someone that I forged ahead without giving the fact that he was married a second thought. He succeeded with my 4 email challenge as posted in my original ad and we ended up exchanging our personal information. Once he gave me his real name and phone number there was no stopping things. His name was Jack and he was a website developer who lived on the East side of Chicago.

One day he called me and asked if I could meet him at the grocery store near where I lived. Back then I didn't have a vehicle so I was not able to meet him where he had originally requested. I was so excited, as soon as I got off of the phone with him, I immediately jumped in the shower, dressed and headed out the door.

As I walked away from my apartment building, I thought to myself, do I really know what I am doing? I definitely knew I was nervous and not sure if I knew how the meet and greet with someone online would or should go in person. I kept thinking about what I would say when I first met him, even as I reached closer to my destination the same thoughts kept circling in my head. His instructions to me were that he would be waiting in his car in the grocery store parking lot. As I entered the parking lot, my eyes immediately began scanning the few vehicles that were parked there. It was just my luck that I noticed there several guys waiting in their cars; I was dumbfounded as to how I would single out my online friend from the others. Everyone must have had an online date I thought to myself.

I decided I would just call Jack to see if I could narrow down which car he was in. His phone rang ten times but he never answered. I then texted him to see if that would get some response from him. By the second text with still no response, I started to become angry thinking he had made me come all that way for nothing. I stood there feeling at odds about what my next move would be and I began to head back in the direction of my apartment. By the time I had walked out of the parking lot and made it to the sidewalk, my phone made a slight chirp alerting me that I had a missed text. He had texted me back a couple minutes after he must have received my last one. When I went into my missed messages folder, I saw that he had responded that he was on his way. As I was deleting his text and starting in on my own response, my phone began to vibrate in my palm. Absentmindedly I had already started to head back toward the grocery store parking lot when I answered the phone.

"Hey, this is Jack, I hope you aren't leaving yet, I am pulling into the parking lot now." My online paramour said. He didn't even wait for a response in return before I heard the dead silence of an ended phone call.

As I was walking into the parking lot alongside the drive entry of the lot He then called a navy blue Lexus drove right past in front of me with its head lights flashing.. I walked slowly and tentatively towards the vehicle which had slowed as it drove into the lot and reached over to open the passenger door while at the same time placing my phone back in my waist holder. The passenger side window was down a third of the way, but the car door was locked. The look on my face must have been one of surprise and confusion all at the same time. As I looked up from the locked door handle to peer into the car at the man that sat behind the wheel of the car looked at me with an equally weird look and speedily drove forward to avoid me attempting another entry into his car.

I was beginning to wonder if this wasn't a subtle sign that I needed to turn around and go back home. But as if on cue, my phone vibrated at my waist once again.

"Ok, I'm here, in the smaller parking lot," Jack said again, still not waiting for a response from me. This time I didn't allow him to hang up before I asked a question of my own.

"Ok, what kind of car are you in?" I asked.

Once I realized he was on the other side of the building from where I was located, I immediately walked the other way fast enough so that I wouldn't meet up face to face with the gentleman in the Lexus who now probably thought I was a car jacker, all the while feeling a bit embarrassed as I walked. When I turned the corner at the other side of the grocery store to enter the smaller lot, my eye immediately caught sight of the car that Jack had described. I approached slowly, not really being able to make out a lot of detail about the man in the driver's seat. When I was close enough I reached for the door and this handle opened easily. As I got into the car I remember having looked all around the parking lot to make sure no one that knew me saw me getting into the car, but all I could see were actual patrons of the store entering and exiting, none of whom I knew. I was still nervous as I settled into the car, but after taking one look finally at the mysterious Jack, much of my nervousness started to wan. To say that Jack was handsome would have been an understatement. I could tell even from him sitting behind the wheel that he had the body of a Greek god with greenish eyes and short blonde hair. He was clean shaven and sported a nice tan to complete the package. He was wearing a tank top that looked like it was about to rip because it fit so snugly against his muscular chest.

As I was continuing to take physical inventory, he suddenly interrupted my thoughts and said confidently, "Don't worry, you may get some when we get to my place. And I already know I get lots of people looking at me like you're doing right now." I was floored at his boldness, but immediately turned on.

I was still caught off guard by his boldness and hadn't responded yet, when he added, "I only do this when my wife can't give me some but I am still a straight man because I'm doing the job and I will never be on the bottom side. I'm a top!"

This was my first time getting an explanation albeit a crude one about what the terms top and bottom meant. I would later learn that the shallow straight types like Jack all believed that as a top they weren't really gay. In Jack's case I believed later he had only said it out of his own shame and guilt.

"Well if you are sleeping with a man you are bisexual as of now," I responded.

"You're young what do you know?" he commented dismissing my statement.

The conversation ended after his statement and we continued to drive in silence. We weren't driving for very long before Jack parked in front of an expensive downtown apartment building indicating that we had reached his place.

I had thought since he made it a point to mention about his wife that we would have entered through an inconspicuous entrance to his building, but instead he walked me right in the front lobby door. As we passed the security office who greeted us, Jack introduced me as his sister's adopted son. I couldn't tell because I didn't see the look on his face as he was telling this to the security guard whether he was being facetious or not. I do recall that my jaw dropped but I closed my mouth just as suddenly and simply said, "Hi," with a smile to the security officer as we walked by heading towards the elevator.

As we both entered the elevator and stood side by side in silence on the way up, I was wondering how exactly the rest of the evening would unfold. I didn't have to wonder for very long, because the minute we entered his apartment, Jack exhibited immediately how the rest of the evening would go by pressing himself against me right in the foyer of his apartment once he had closed the door. I knew better than to say anything, this is what I was here for and at least he was to the point and ready to go. He was all over me, kissing me deeply and grabbing my ass with his hands as he pressed me up and into him. He was bigger and taller than me so he used that to his advantage to force me further down the hall, removing my clothes and his as we hug walked down the hall with my back towards the destination. I just wanted to enjoy the feel of his ripped muscles on my skin and under my hands. Suddenly I felt the immovable pressure of a closed door on my back, but that didn't stop him from kissing me and continuing to rub my ass, instead he moved one hand and swiftly opened the door behind me. Before I could take in the new surroundings of his bedroom, he lifted me, walked me over and threw me right on his bed. I was more than turned on by his masculine take charge energy and I reveled in the fact that no words needed to be said to explain what we were doing. As I laid there watching him get underdressed I glimpsed from the corner of my right eye a photo of a man who was presumably Jack and woman in front of outdoor scenery. In the heat of the moment I had forgotten Jack was married and from the looks of the photo happily married or at least his wife thought so. And here I was in the same bed he slept with his wife. Jack could tell the mood had changed, I didn't feel comfortable at all. It was quite disrespectful to know that I was violating his wife's space like that and thoroughly mess up her sheets in the process, the least I could do was to give her that much respect I mean I was about to sleep with her man.

So we took things into the kitchen on the counter instead. There it happened, our bodies intertwined with me and the upper part of my body lying across the counter, my ass in the air with his hands on either side of my waist as he began thrusting fast and hard. It was so intense and as I was beginning to climax, my moaning was getting louder like when waves build up and begin roaring just before night. I was about to climax all over the European wood front cabinets when suddenly the telephone that was located on the wall next to the countertop which had become my temporary bed, rang. Given my bent over position and limited view of what he was about to do, I was floored when he answered it on the second ring! I could tell immediately who it was just from his vague responses, it was his wife and apparently she was on her way home but with company as well. I didn't know whether to dislodge his hard dick from my ass and get out of there or wait patiently until he finished his little chat with the wife. Again he made the decision for the both of us
with little argument from me. It was as though he hadn't just spoken with his wife when he returned his attention back to my waiting ass. He started back in slow and built up,

when he did climax with every grunt I could feel him go deeper into me, which in turn made me climax.

8

Coming out of Nigeria and living in the US a nation where freedom is sometimes taken for advantage, was the best gift I could have ever received.

I could now speak my mind. I mean where else can someone say on national television, that the President of their country doesn't care about Black people? In Nigeria that could never happen on a national event without the person being arrested. Here people could get married in one day and divorced that same very same day. You could choose to going into whatever field of work you wanted to without needing permission to do so or without being concerned about what someone else thought about that field of work. I was determined when I came back to the US to exercise my freedoms to the fullest extent. A part of me remained in Nigeria when I came back, that part of me that was sweet, innocent and felt like I wanted to find and share my life with one lover. Here I was interested in not only experiencing daily freedoms but in my sexual freedom as well. I ended up living in Chicago to attend college, and to further my education and it was in Chicago that the most significant chapter in my life Commenced. There were times when it felt as though I was dumped in the city of Chicago to fend for myself and make my way up the ladder of life. It was in Chicago that my search for love sometimes mirrored a nightmare of an unstoppable addiction. I came to Chicago as Tunde, and would turn into someone totally different after everything was said and done.

My days in Chicago were spent as a student, attending classes, hanging out and getting acclimated to big city life. . Sex for me was like a drug and so it seemed for my partners as well, once they had been with me, they were addicted and always came back for more. The number of times that I had sex with random men was uncountable just like sand. . It seemed as though because I had no limitations to the things that I would do sexually many of the men I met online and otherwise sought to fulfill their fantasies with me. The words "yes, ok, or I will" from my lips made men rush to my door step in seconds. I would always use the same screen names and simply rotate the ones I would use dependent on the website; which were African Obsession, Black Booty Gum or African Sexiness.

I would log on and my private message page would have so many messages that I wouldn't be able to keep up with or track who I had answered or who I hadn't. . If I responded to a message I would get a reply within seconds. The mailbox got full which was very rare for the website. The word cyber stalker got its meaning from my page when many got obsessed that if I said I wasn't interested they would make many more numerous profiles just to get to me. There were some men who wrote full essays in my inbox but in brief summary it was always just about what they dreamed of doing to me. It was funny when online a guy came across as a thug in his profile, but became a total professional when they messaged me; they made sure they spoke proper English all the while using slang in their profile. I wouldn't say that I had a particular type, but for me the ones who were models, body builders, or just every day handsome all still had to work just as hard as every other person that took a chance and messaged me. This doesn't mean that I didn't use some sort of discrimination when selecting because there were some who definitely got no's. Some said I was conceited but I felt I was just playing the game like everyone else online was at that time. The entire internet scene became like a foray to a shopping mall for me; there were lots of products to choose from and then there were days when I simply window shopped.

9

I ended up passing by Jack's wife and their guest in the hall as I was leaving their apartment. Before I left Jack gave me money for cab fare as though he were tipping me for my performance. I left his apartment and walked out the door saying goodbye to him over my shoulder, knowing that I was not going to see him again. The only way I was able to recognize his wife was from recall of the photo on the nightstand next to the bed. She was walking down the hall with a police officer heading in my direction. I wondered if they had seen the exact door I emerged from as they both walked passed me. They seemed to be enjoying their conversation as they were both laughing as they walked past. There was something familiar and recognizable about the Police Officer that was walking with her, and not because of any arrest in my past. I kept thinking about where I knew him from as I got onto the elevator to do downstairs.

Then I had figured it out! He was someone who I had also chatted with online! I started to smile knowingly; in his profile he was wearing checkered blue and white boxers with his face in full view. He was on one of the sites I was a member of called, Black Gay Conversation. Black Gay Conversation was a website that was mainly geared towards the black GLBT community. There were guys on there that were even straight but identified as being just curious. Even though anyone could join, there were primarily young black men on the site. . I preferred Black Gay Conversation compared to Carmen list because it felt somewhat safer because it was a requirement for people to have their photos up to be able to converse with others on the site. Also it made it easier to converse with someone when you knew what they looked like and who it is you were talking to from the beginning.

What really had me amazed was that I had skipped over the police officer to meet up with Jack instead. He must have lied to me I thought to myself online he had said that he worked at a casino and yet here he was wearing a policeman's uniform. I wondered how or who he was in relation to Jack and his wife. I made a mental note to ask Jack if we made contact and maybe talked later online. By the time I made it downstairs and had called a cab I had decided instead I was simply going to message the police officer directly on his profile once I got home because I thought it was highly unlikely I would ever hear from Jack.

I got off at the lobby and headed towards the front entrance doors. I still needed to call a cab but I would do once I was outside of the building. Once I called the cab, I sat waiting on one of the front benches which sat along the building. I must have been deep in my thoughts because I didn't even see when, Mr. Blue & White Checkered shorts was approaching me.

"Don't I know you from BGC?" he asked tentatively. His question was met with both my surprise and raised eyebrows. "Your name online is Ayo?"

I was surprised he had recognized me in the quick moment he had walked by me with Jack's wife. "Uh…BGC?" I asked back, not wanting to acknowledge too much too soon.

"Yeah," he said whispering and glancing around this time. "Black Gay Conversation," he added.

"Oh yeah," I responded with a measure of guilt. "Now I remember you."

"My real name is K," he continued. "What are you doing out here?"

"I was just visiting a friend," I said lying immediately. "Your name is just Kay?" I asked, thinking he was spelling it like a woman's name.

"Yeah man just call me K," he said emphasizing it was just the letter K he was going by in instead of an entire name.

"My real name is Tunde," I said in return.

K stood standing about 6'3" feet tall, well built and handsome. I took a quick glance at the front of his slacks and I could tell he was well endowed to say the least. He stayed there talking to me about light topics and told me he lived in Brickton Park which was a suburb on the other side from where I lived. By the time my cab had come we had exchanged phone numbers and agreed to give one another a call to hang out at a later time.

By the time I reached home, I was happy simply not to have to answer any of my roommates' questions about my whereabouts because he hadn't gotten in yet. It wasn't until several weeks later that Kay and I made contact again. One thing I was sure of, he was a lot of work once I began to know him better. I decided to take a different approach with K, so I let him know how I felt about wanting to be in a relationship and what I was looking for in that person. I remember he told me at that time he was searching for the one as well and had no problem with my age and the fact that I was younger than him.

He was also honest in the beginning and disclosed that he was bisexual, was opening to dating and didn't like games or drama when it came to relationships. At the time, it seemed like it would be an easy relationship and worth my time to pursue.

From day one, K was always difficult to get a hold of, even to simply say hello by phone. He rarely returned calls which became more and more frustrating for me as things progressed. Even though he was hard to reach in person, I noticed that whenever I went online to Black Gay Conversation he would also be online. I would have to message him to get in contact with him and those were the only times he would reply as expected. There were times when I would call and he would pick up the phone and say he was busy and would call back in a few minutes which usually turned out to be three days later. I offered going all the way to go see him even though his place was too far but he always had some excuse that he had to work or his family was visiting. I started to pull back after a few weeks to give him space and to reassess what exactly I was wanting from K.

One day when I was finally able to corner him about spending time together, he agreed to come over and see me.

We were parked outside of my apartment since my roommate was at home and I wanted to be able to talk to him in private. But instead of talking, I could tell from his body language and the way he had placed his hand on my knee and was gently squeezing, exactly what K had come over to do. And there was something in me that wanted to please him to make him realize that I really liked him. That night, in order to please him I went with the flow, I bent over and let him tickle my tonsils the way he liked.

It wasn't as though Kay was selfish sexually, after I gave him what he needed, he in turn grabbed my member between his hands. That night he made me reach climax right there in his car for all the worlds to see, the evidence was clear in his hands. His wide palms took all that I had released and he reached over afterwards and cleaned it off with a tissue that he had in his car. And that was it. I smiled and he immediately leaned over to kiss me. When I was getting out of his car, there were some passersby that looked in my direction, I wasn't sure if they knew what had just happened but I didn't care even if they did. I was way too happy thinking about the fact that I had at least done something good to make him stay a bit longer this time. Although the reunion between us ended up being short lived, because the next month he started to pull back away from me again the his excuse was that he was busy as usual, except this time he deleted his profile online so I wasn't able to reach him there when I couldn't get him on the phone. I wondered why, but I never asked him.

I never saw K again. Well once I did remember seeing him, except this time, he was back online in the visitor section of an 18 year olds profile on one of the sites I usually checked out. It was the same photo he had sent me in is blue and white checkered boxer shorts.

10

Even with my success rate not being quite where I wanted it to be in my search for love online, I remained faithful to my search. A month so after my last interaction with K, I answered an ad entitled _**'Great looking professional man looking for a cool guy'**_. It didn't take very long before I received a response, it was right around the two hour mark. The only thing in is response was his inquiry about my stats and location in Chicago. I responded telling him I was 19 and lived on the north side of Chicago. He didn't seem to be bothered by my age but rather more bothered that I wasn't responding fast enough. We made several attempts to hook up but our schedules never matched and then I also began a part time job. A few months passed with us only communicating on the internet until we finally coordinated a convenient time when we were both able to meet up. It was early on a Monday morning before we both had to go in to work. For some reason it wasn't until that morning I asked him for a description of what he looked like.

"I don't have a picture but trust me I am very handsome," he said.

In response, I gave him my address and waited patiently for his call to alert me he was close. It was approximately an hour and half later before he called to let me know he was downstairs.

"I am wearing blue jeans and a black polo shirt, where are you?" he asked when I had picked up the call. When I got downstairs in front of my apartment, he was easy to spot; he was the only guy standing on the street right beside a car looking curiously in my direction. As I walked towards him, I took in the full picture of my new friend. He was 6'4", white with a full beard, jet black hair which you could tell had been dyed which was slicked back with gel. He was wearing reading glasses which were pulled down on his nose and beneath the glasses he had freckles which covered his T zone.

As I walked towards him he outstretched his hand and said, "Hi, I'm Leo."

"I'm Tunde," I replied reaching for his hand.

"What a strange name," he said teasingly. "I hear an

accent, where are you from?" he asked.

"I'm from Africa," I replied smiling.

He must have seen the nervous look on my face as I was looking up and down my street. I really didn't feel like answering any questions from my roommate about the identity of my new friend.

"Are you ok?" he asked.

"You need to relax because I'm really laid back," he added.

I started to smile and relaxed a little so I wouldn't scare him off. "Is it ok if we go for a drive?" I suggested.

"Sure that sounds like a good idea," he said turning around to open the passenger door for me.

I started to feel more comfortable and relaxed as he drove away from my place.

"So how long have you been on Carmenslist?" he asked.

"Not too long I'm pretty much a newbie," I said, slightly stretching the truth.

"Fresh meat, I see," he responded.

I giggled and looked in his direction. He must have taken my laughter as his cue to then grab my hand and place it on his lap. I wasn't quite ready to get busy in this guys car, so I asked, "Can we wait until we get to your place?"

He laughed in response and said, "Ok then newbie."

It wasn't long before we had reached his place but it seemed to be a bit faster than I needed it to be just then. I had no time to think about how I wanted to proceed with him. I simply followed behind as he led the way to his apartment. When we entered his apartment, I was impressed by the furnishings and mood that he had set for his home.

"Would you like something to drink or do you want to bend over right away?" he asked with confidence, seeming sure of what my answer would be to his question.

I must have looked at him with a crazy look because then he began to laugh. I couldn't blame him for such a distasteful joke, after all that's what he brought me here for, it's what they all usually brought me back to their place for in the end. And the ad *was* under the "no strings attached" section, which in the beginning I didn't know what was entailed. Even still, I thought that through the sex I could reach him and still have hopes of a relationship. We settled down on his couch in front of the TV in the living room.

He looked at me and said, "You need to relax, maybe take some clothes off and just feel free man." I went ahead and did as he suggested and took of my polo shirt and shoes leaving my tank top and jeans on. I was still hopeful that this first meeting might go well so I waited to see if he would ask if I was single or had a boy friend. I mean for me that was a sign that they possibly had interest in me beyond sex. In other words they would want to see me beyond a simple one night stand. We sat there on his couch making light conversation and watching the program on TV.

"What time do you have to be at work?" I asked.

"I can go in when I want," he responded. "I am one of the managers."

"Good," I said, thinking that indeed this meeting would definitely be different. He actually seemed to want to know more about me and just converse.

"What about you, what time do I have to have you back?" he asked in turn. I glanced at my watch, actually having forgotten that I still needed to make it in to work.

"I still have a good three hours," I said. "I will still be on time to work if you get me back in about two and a half hours."

"Ok," he said. "That works for me."

Before I could get into asking him another question about himself, his cell phone rang. He picked it up on the second ring and excused himself to go speak in private. Immediately I thought back to Jack and his wife calling just as we were having sex. I was sure this wasn't the case this time; he hadn't mentioned anything about a wife in person or in any of his emails. I could hear bits and pieces of the conversation as he spoke from the other room. But I could only surmise was being said to him by the way he responded. It definitely was not a wife, because I could hear him describing me to the unknown called. Must be a friend checking in on him I thought as I settled back into the couch, pushing the wife thoughts away. When he had ended his call and returned to the couch, he announced that someone was coming over.

"Oh ok, one of your friends?" I asked.

"Yes, he forgot some stuff at my place and he needs it for some mtg.," he said.

"Cool, I get to meet one of your friends," I said. "That will tell me more about you," I said smiling.

"Yeah, something like that," he responded absently.

Not more than thirty minutes had passed before there was a knock at his apartment door. I could hear him greeting his new guest as they walked into the living room. In walked a tall black man with pure smooth skin. His skin was light and had a ripped look to it with his scruffy beard and bald cut.

"Tunde, this is my friend Aaron," Leo introduced.

"Nice to meet you," I said outstretching my arm.

"Wow, he is as handsome as you described," Aaron said looking at me with more interest than I was comfortable.

"Thank you," I said, a little caught off guard by the

compliment.

"You get an A for this one," continued Aaron.

"What..?" was all I managed before Leo jumped into the conversation finally.

"I told you," he said. "Don't worry Tunde, you are still a newbie, you will learn."

All of a sudden, I felt helpless; I couldn't believe this situation I had gotten myself into. I was being expected to have sex with not just one, but both of these men. I felt as though I didn't have a choice to back out of the situation, I had voluntarily placed myself in. It was my fault.

"Well relax boy this won't hurt I promise," Aaron said.

They laid me on the bed and his friend started first. I felt the whole time while he was pounding into me as thought my body would burst. He was too big and I began to make loud noises because it was painful, but oddly pleasuring at the same time. . Something I called sexual pain.

That day I never did have sex with Leo. Something told me he just wanted to watch my encounter with Aaron in the first place. I had been set up, but somehow I wasn't angry. I had actually enjoyed the pleasure and pain that I experienced with Aaron. I even received a text from him the next day which read, "Good morning babe I'm so happy I met you yesterday, I want you to be mine for real, let me love you". Something inside me was excited. Maybe this could be the real thing. Even having met him under those circumstances, it could be love. There were tons of people who had met under stranger occasions and could look back on it and laugh years later I thought. Like any other person in hopes of happiness and love I replied to the text message instantly. My text reply got a phone call in return and he asked if he could come over to my place. I had to work that day but I have longed so much for love and a relationship, I decided fulfilling his request would get me what I wanted in the end, so I cancelled work to see him. He came over after he got off of work unlike me who had called in and cancelled work. It was approximately 6pm when he came over. The door bell rang and I went to open the door downstairs with only a robe on with nothing under it. It was my kind of way to get a man to notice the fact that I was interested and ready to fulfill every request. When I opened the door he leaned over and gave me a kiss. How sweet I thought to myself as I was living in the moment. I walked him upstairs and directed him into my room. We both sat down on my bed and there was an unusual silence for a few seconds. It was kind of awkward I thought to myself, I really only knew this guy's name. Aaron had a bag in his hand which contained alcohol. I went to the kitchen and got him a cup so he could have a drink. I never drank alcohol so I didn't feel the need to bring two. As he poured himself a drink, I removed my robe so he could fully admire my body. I enjoyed showing my body to please whoever I was with; I needed that look of approval and admiration. I could tell from the way he was smiling behind his cup as he drank that he liked what he saw.

There was no ceremony in the manner that he quickly stood, turned me around and bent me over. I was used to this position and knew how to assume it well. Aaron was so far into his own pleasure moment that he didn't notice or hear me saying that I wanted to stop. I kept on trying to push him away from behind me but it was a bit too late when I found myself falling straight to the floor. This was my first time fainting ever in my life. When I was able to open my eyes, all I could see was a dark shadowed figure standing over me. As my eyes began to focus and adjust I noticed it was Aaron tapping me on my shoulder and asking "Are you ok man?"

I sat up and said "Yeah, I think so."

"Man you scared the hell out of me." Aaron said.

I began to get up but felt very weak and was sweating profusely. My throat felt dry. Aaron walked out the room and found his way into my kitchen to get me some water. He walked in with the water and I took a slow and steady sip. At least he was showing concern I thought to myself.

"Hey, I have to go, but I want to make sure you are ok," he added.

Nodding, I sat up further on my bed. "Yes, I think I'm ok, maybe I was just so excited to see you," I said, not really sure about why I had fainted. My comment won a big grin from him in return.

He then asked, "Hey do you think I can get a few dollars to use for some gas money and food?"

You would think that in my condition that he would have avoided such a question and would only be concerned about me feeling better. But I really wanted to see him again, so I reached over to get my wallet and handed him a twenty. He grabbed the money from me and started to get dressed.

"You're leaving now?" I asked with a tone of sadness and a mixture of disappointment.

"Yeah man, I gotta go pick up my friend," was his response.

"Alright man, I'm happy to see you're feeling better, I'll call you later." Even in my semi dizzy state, I knew what he really meant, was thank you for the ass.

When Aaron left, I lied on the floor still winded and a little dizzy. At that time I wasn't concerned about anything serious being wrong with me, it just seemed like a fluke occurrence which I soon forgot about.

11

Even though I spent the majority of my free and what was supposed to be dedicated time on the internet. I did manage to make friendships along the way which helped keep me sane in the midst of my entanglements. I had two really good friends when I first started delving into the world of cyber relationships, Michael and Bryan. Bryan and I met on campus one day at school and eventually ended up working at the same retail store as well. Bryan introduced me to his friend Michael and we all started to hang out together. We had an ongoing Friday night ritual of hanging out. We would watch a movie, have dinner or cruise around Boy's Village in Chicago.

We would make a big production of things, by meeting up at my place to get dressed up; at times we would even bring extra clothing on our outings in case someone wanted to change their shirt or pants to complete their look.

None of us were of age to go into the clubs but we still managed to get in thanks to Bryan who seemed to know all the bouncers and security personally.

Even though I wasn't a drinker, I would order something that looked like a drink so I could blend in with the other patrons in the clubs. I would stand against the wall with Michael and Bryan boy watching, chatting and giggling about some guy that had caught our eye in the club. Sometimes I would dance if asked.

One of my passions was dancing. As soon as I got to Chicago I had joined with a local all male, gay dance troupes. It made me feel good to dance. I would sometimes invite Michael and Bryan to our performances as well. They would always show up to give their support and never missed a show that I invited them to come and see.

Eventually my friendship with Bryan and Michael would end. I had never experienced the catty side of the community when it came to friendships as yet. I had a sexual interlude with a guy I had met online and we had started dating for a brief period afterwards. I was head over heels for the guy and had introduced him to Bryan one night when we were all hanging out. We continued seeing each other and one night while I was over at his house, I got nosey and picked up his cell phone while he was in the shower.

I saw several text messages from him and Bryan arranging to see each other to 'get it in' according to the text. I was so hurt and disappointed that not even friendships were sacred when it came to protecting your relationship. I approached Bryan about it, because I figured I didn't expect very much from a guy I had met over the internet, but from my friend I did.

"Its life, get over it Tunde," he had said.

"But we are friends, why would you disrespect me like that?" I asked.

"I'm not up for the drama, either you can get over it or you can't," he finished and hung up the phone on me.

I couldn't get over it and I never forgot about it. It wasn't until I met my friends Sammy and John that I allowed anyone from the community to get that close enough to me to call themself my friend.

My other passion asides form dancing was volunteering. I would see an ad or a notice on campus about an organization looking for helpers and I would jump at the opportunity. I always knew that volunteering could lead to other things if I put my heart into it. The Critical Care Center was one of the places that I volunteered at and it was also my favorite. There were quite a few seniors who were being cared for at the center and there were also people who had suffered a traumatic injury who weren't able to be cared for at home who were housed there.

When I walked into the Center it made me feel as though I was in a loved place. The smiles they had on their faces when I arrived made me feel welcomed and wanted. Dependent on what capacity they needed me on the days that I was schedule I would be doing anything from assisting the staff in the kitchen in preparing meals to reading to patients and helping them complete their daily routines. It's one of the ways that I learned how to cook different American meals.

As a volunteer we weren't supposed to have favorite patients but I did anyway. His name was Eddie; I think I liked him because he had a wonderful heart. He was 29 and was going to have to live the rest of his life in a wheel chair due to a climbing accident. I had later found out from one the staff at the center that because of his injuries he was brought to the center by his fiancé who said she could no longer care for him. She never returned after signing off on the papers to admit him. One time I was helping him get dressed and settled into his chair for the day. As I bent over to adjust his arms properly, he leaned in and gave me a peck on the cheek. I was surprised and taken aback when he said, "You are amazing, any guy would be lucky to have you."

"You think so?" I asked smiling.

"Hey if I were gay, I would marry you," he said laughing at my reaction to his peck.

We would sit in his room and talk about how much joy climbing would gave him when he was still able to do it. I tried teaching him some Yoruba but it always came out sounding garbled when he tried to pronounce some of the words. We would laugh because we both knew he was never going to be really good at it, but he tried just the same.

Those words gave me more hope than he knew. At that time, I was in the midst of my many hook-ups and starting to lose hope that I would ever find someone to just settle down with and be happy. Eddie eventually died from his injuries that he had suffered, for a while I couldn't find the joy to keep working there. I told the volunteer coordinator that my school schedule was getting hectic so I wouldn't' have to go back. I did go back after a while, but it wasn't the same, I felt like I had lost a good friend.

12

I went to bed that night thinking how great of a night it was with Aaron, well asides from my fainting spell and the temporary loan I had given him. I wondered why he hadn't called that same night to see how I was doing but I excused it away, thinking he may have decided to go hang out with friends and gotten sidetracked. About a week had passed, I kept myself busying going about my usual business of going attending classes, working and any other activities I decided to be engaged to that week. I was glued to my cell phone during the off times in case Aaron decided to send me a message, I didn't want to miss an opportunity to spend some time with him. But that week there weren't many texts that came from him.

That Friday, I called him since I noticed he wasn't contacting me like he had before, which I had to admit was bothering me. Finally when I was able to reach him, I complained about my unhappiness with the lack of communication. He acquiesced and we planned to meet up the next day, which was Saturday morning. From early that morning, I was focused on making sure that I looked good for him. I even went to the braiding shop to get my hair twisted in a dred lock style. Afterwards, I even went shopping to buy a new outfit. I made sure and shaved and did all the necessary grooming which I always did when I felt good about a particular person I was to meet.

I was standing downstairs in front of my apartment when he arrived in his red sports car with his music bumping loud. He looked so sexy behind the wheel of his car, but I tried to play it cool as he pulled up to the curb in front of me. I was surprised when he hopped out from the car, walked across to the passenger side of the car and opened the door for me to get in. He waited for me to settle into the seat and put on my seatbelt before shutting to door closed. As he got in and drove off I just sat there beside him blushing in the dimly light car. For me the night was perfect so far, I felt I had the right guy beside me who seemed to be doing the perfect things. He ended up taking me to a beach close by, where we parked and took a walk across the boardwalk that ran along the side of the beach. Even though by now I labeled myself gay and somewhat out, I still didn't feel comfortable holding a guys hand. I was always afraid of what people would say when they saw two guys together in that manner. And in some ways it seemed rather wrong to me to be walking so close to another man in public, I wasn't sure if that was just part of my strict African upbringing rearing its head.

As I was admonishing myself about whether to hold his hand or not, a woman and her male companion walked by us. She said "You two look great together," and smiled at us as she walked by.

I didn't think she knew that I was a man. With my hair in braids I could pass for a woman unless you were looking closely enough to tell otherwise. But I still enjoyed her compliment about us just the same. As we walked, there was a breeze was softly brushing against me. He moved closer to me as we walked still not touching me, and it felt good. When we got to the end of the pier, he stopped and turned me towards him so that he could place a light kiss on my lips. For me this sealed deal. That kiss, took my breath away, it was what I had been waiting for, someone to take what it was I wanted seriously. After he kissed me, he gave me a gentle bear hug which I feigned to not want and we began tussling a little and play fighting there at the end of the pier. I was happy there weren't other people nearby us to know what we were doing. , He suggested that we go down to the actual beach so that we could sit and talk. When we made it the bottom of the pier, he cleared a little area in the sand for me to sit.

We lay on the sand and talked about what was going on with our respective lives at the moment. It seemed as though he wanted for both of us to put things on the table regarding where we were at in our lives. That was when he told me that he was a stripper and was his main and only means of survival. He said he mostly performed at the gay bars and also did private dancing requests.

I didn't feel as though I had any rights to judge what his occupation was, so long as he wasn't asking me to sit there and watch as he danced for other men, I was fine with his choice of careers. Who was I to judge right at that moment? I mean at least he came forward and told me the truth. I also had secrets of my own but I was sure that I wasn't planning on disclosing them to him just then. I did disclose to him that I was also a performer and not just any performer but a drag performer. Even though I wasn't a stripper I was still a drag performer that could understand another person's love for performing on stage. I also went on and told him that I was studying graphic design. I even shared with him some of my design ideas which I had saved on my phone.

He then asked, "So with all of your talents, are you really good at any of them?"

I replied smartly, "If I was in the right state you would have already heard my name on TV for all of my talents."

He said the drag didn't bother him but that it was new to him "What's your stripper name?" I asked, putting the focus back on him.

"Tornado Cane," he responded.

I giggled when he said it and I could tell immediately that I had offended him. I simply couldn't understand why someone would give themselves a name that sounded like a weather forecast.

"Sorry for laughing," I said.

"What's so funny?" he asked.

"I'm sorry, it just sounds like hurricane, and I pictured you doing this weird circular dance on a stage someplace," I said.

He started to laugh himself, which I felt relieved about, I didn't want to offend him, but I did think it was a funny name. We sat there talking about my school, his work and life in general. We would have been out there talking a lot longer, but it started to get dark and we decided to continue our conversation at a later time. I was pleasantly surprised by the simple evening I had with Aaron, considering the manner in which we had met. I was happy for the small advances I had made towards once and for all finding someone just for me.

13

The next time I was able to jump on the Adam 4 Steve website again, I was not surprised to see that as usual my inbox mail was full. I knew the boys who hit me up online all wanted more but not all men were able enough to handle me and stay for what I really wanted and could offer which was love. I knew many men, straight and gay that ran away from that word, love. The great thing to me about Adam 4 Steve was that it had options so every user could be specific about what it was they were seeking and they would automatically know what the person contacting them was looking for in a potential date. The 'looking for' section had options like, 1 on 1 sex, friendship, relationship, miscellaneous fetishes, 3some/group sex and cam2cam. The 'body type options' included slim, average, swimmers, athletic, muscular, bodybuilder and large. The 'scene options' listed were casual, conservative, alternative, drag, leather, military, jock, trendy and punk. The 'sexual role option' that you had to have on your status before anyone would be allowed to continue communicating with someone they were interested in, was bottom, top, versatile, oral, versatile/top or versatile/bottom... Sometimes when I went on there, it almost felt like a virtual male vending machine store.

Even though my permanent search was for a soul mate, there were times when I simply wanted to get my needs met. Joe was that person for me for awhile. He stood 6'3 feet tall, weighed 205, had a muscular build and smooth skin. He was 35yrs old or so he told while we were still chatting online, until we met in person and he told me he was really 45. His profile title read *'Coming to dick you down'.* With a title like that, I couldn't help but to make contact with him. Joe was a person that would make you question any straight male in a three piece suit if they were gay or not. By his appearance he seemed absolutely alpha male and as though he would punch you if you if another male came onto him. Joe knew all the tricks of the trade to giving great sex. I was proud that someone with my experience was able to handle what he brought to the bedroom. I didn't know much about his personal life, until one time when we were having one of our all night sweat sessions, he yelled, "You take it better than my wife!!!"

Needless to say that session was ruined, but I didn't stop from seeing him. He must have always removed his wedding ring whenever he came to see me, because I never knew he was married until that moment. Men like Joe made me ask questions like which would a wife rather deal with, her man cheating on her with a man or a woman.

Joe came more than a few times a week to my place and

eventually told me that he had kids as well. He was so desperate to have sex sometimes that one more than one occasion he had shown up to my place and had people waiting in his car while he had his fun upstairs with me.

Did I care about how or when he came over? Definitely not, because as far as I knew I was just a sex option for him and he wasn't my priority at that time either.

It was around this time that I began to simply go with the flow in meeting men and of not caring about the outcome because the gay scene was just as it is. It didn't feel like the normal me to be like this but it was one of the only ways I was at least successful in blocking my emotions from getting me involved with someone. Joe didn't even care if my roommate was at home or not he still would come over any way if he had time in his schedule and could get away from his wife without her wondering about where he was at night.

Joe always made it clear what he wanted from me and I was fine with it. He once called me to tell me how he wanted to bring someone over to fuck me, so he could watch for his satisfaction. I'm surprised he felt comfortable enough talking to me like that in his office within earshot of his assistant. He would be telling me about his need to spread my ass cheeks and pump his manhood into me.

The great thing about Joe was that being with him made me want to research more and hone my sexual skills. In my own way of seeking out that ultimate love I thought that of all things a man would stay for in a relationship, great sex would be first then would be the personality.

14

I must admit I have had my share of parasites in relationships. I was smart enough each time to not stay with them for very long, or at the worst case to have online relationships only with these types. After the first encounter with a parasite, I was able to spot them more quickly and head them off at the onset before I could get dragged down and hurt. Sometimes I would use random screen names to make sure I could shake someone off who was beginning to get too close or ask for too much. I always tried to make a unique screen name or have initials that were close to a screen name I used before. 'Black Booty Gum' was one of my names that I used. I came up with that name because I had a black butt and to me when I was dressed it looked like it was packed in a bubble gum packaging. Of course online everyone I spoke with had a nasty translation for the screen name. A guy with the online screen name Bentleydude was one of the people I kept at bay by only having online contact with him.

Bentleydude@ymail.com (6/12/2009 3:29:12 AM): hey

BBG (6/12/2009 3:29:20 AM): hey

Bentleydude@ymail.com (6/12/2009 3:30:02 AM): so what's up baby?

bentleydude@ymail.com (6/12/2009 3:30:19 AM): can I see some more ass?

BBG (6/12/2009 3:30:34 AM): be careful with that word

bentleydude@ymail.com (6/12/2009 3:30:52 AM): what word?

BBG (6/12/2009 3:30:56 AM): baby

bentleydude@ymail.com (6/12/2009 3:31:06 AM): WHATEVER

bentleydude@ymail.com (6/12/2009 3:31:25 AM): SHOW ME SOME ASS

bentleydude@ymail.com (6/12/2009 3:32:35 AM): YOU HAVE WEB CAM?

BBG (6/12/2009 3:32:40 AM): you for real about this?

bentleydude@ymail.com (6/12/2009 3:32:49 AM): YES SIR

BBG (6/12/2009 3:32:56 AM): we'll see

bentleydude@ymail.com (6/12/2009 3:33:05 AM): YES WE WILL

BBG (6/12/2009 3:33:32 AM): cool can I see more pics

bentleydude@ymail.com (6/12/2009 3:33:39 AM): NO!!

BBG (6/12/2009 3:33:43 AM): why?

bentleydude@ymail.com (6/12/2009 3:34:01 AM): BECAUSE I AM NOT REALLY OUT YET

BBG (6/12/2009 3:34:24 AM): oh but u put "out" on your profile

Toby said he lived in California and told me he was a music producer for an artist in Chicago. He never put up a photo on his profile the whole time we communicated online. He did send me a picture by way of email. He was very attractive, had a great body, and a caramel complexion. He said he was a former dancer/stripper and had two sons. When we first started communication, he had just separated from his wife.

About three days later our conversation online began again:

bentleydude@ymail.com (6/15/2009 12:22:18 AM): hey

BBG (6/15/2009 12:22:36 AM): hold on'

bentleydude@ymail.com (6/15/2009 12:24:59 AM): SO IS THE PHOTO I SENT YOU WORKING?

BBG (6/15/2009 12:25:08 AM): I am checking it out now

bentleydude@ymail.com (6/15/2009 12:25:40 AM): ARE YOU MY DUDE?

BBG (6/15/2009 12:25:49 AM): What?

bentleydude@ymail.com (6/15/2009 12:26:06 AM): ARE YOU MY DUDE???

BBG (6/15/2009 12:26:24 AM): yeah why u asking

bentleydude@ymail.com (6/15/2009 12:26:44 AM): I JUST WANT 2 NO

BBG (6/15/2009 12:26:56 AM): oh u sure that's all?

bentleydude@ymail.com (6/15/2009 12:26:59 AM): DO YOU WANT ME?

BBG (6/15/2009 12:27:09 AM): I really do but

bentleydude@ymail.com (6/15/2009 12:27:25 AM): BUT WHAT?

BBG (6/15/2009 12:27:26 AM): do you want me as well?

bentleydude@ymail.com (6/15/2009 12:27:45 AM): YES I WANT YOU TO LOVE ME

He boasted most of the time about how he could have many guys perform by way of webcam for him, whenever I refused. He said he had an ex that almost committed suicide because of him. It was his needless boasting that was a part of him that was not all that interesting to me. Our online conversations kept me busy and entertained when I didn't have someone in real life to entertain. Then in one of our conversations, he stated that if I wanted to be with him I needed to be taking care of him financially because he had bills to pay and other kids aside from the ones he had told me about. I looked at the screen and thought I would have to be crazy to fall for a guy who was 54 years old, had 5 kids in total and would depend on someone half his age to take care of him and his kids. He even went so far as to beg me to give him at least $100.

BBG (7/9/2009 3:17:53 PM): hey

bentleydude@ymail.com (7/9/2009 3:18:20 PM): hey you

BBG (7/9/2009 3:18:35 PM): forgot my name lol

bentleydude@ymail.com (7/9/2009 3:19:01 PM): NO

bentleydude@ymail.com (7/9/2009 3:19:31 PM): What's up WITH YOU?

BBG (7/9/2009 3:20:23 PM): nothing much

BBG (7/9/2009 3:20:31 PM): just staying alive for real

bentleydude@ymail.com (7/9/2009 3:20:49 PM): SEND ME SOME MONEY, MY SON IS IN JAIL

BBG (7/9/2009 3:20:59 PM): what happened?

bentleydude@ymail.com (7/9/2009 3:21:24 PM): I DONT KNOW I AM ON MY WAY THERE NOW

BBG (7/9/2009 3:21:41 PM): wow

BBG (7/9/2009 3:21:43 PM): omg

BBG (7/9/2009 3:21:47 PM): i'm sorry about that

BBG (7/9/2009 3:21:50 PM): how old is he?

bentleydude@ymail.com (7/9/2009 3:22:00 PM): SO I NEED SOME

MONEY

BBG (7/9/2009 3:22:25 PM): lost my job

BBG (7/9/2009 3:22:31 PM): been tough

BBG (7/9/2009 3:23:04 PM): depending on my buddy

BBG (7/9/2009 3:24:53 PM): what are you doing online you need to be on your way to see your son

bentleydude@ymail.com (7/9/2009 3:26:36 PM): I AM

It wasn't long before I blocked him from messaging me any further. The same week I blocked Tony, I met another guy similar to him. His real name was Vie and he lived in Amsterdam.

Vie was so focused on sex there was no other topics that mattered to him. I always made attempts to keep his mind of sex with other topics but we always went back to it. There were times I missed classes or work because I was online chatting with him; there were also much more crazy things I did because I *was* talking on line to him.

BBG (6/18/2009 11:48:00 AM): I MISS U

Roe grand (6/18/2009 11:48:11 AM): awww

BBG (6/18/2009 11:48:14 AM): just had to say that lol

Roe grand (6/18/2009 11:48:19 AM): ok what have you been doing with your body?

BBG (6/18/2009 11:48:42 AM): did u think of me?

Roe grand (6/18/2009 11:48:48 AM): yeah

BBG (6/18/2009 11:49:18 AM): nothing, really at work

Roe grand (6/18/2009 11:49:32 AM): you should go to the gym

BBG (6/18/2009 11:50:42 AM): why?

Roe grand (6/18/2009 11:51:16 AM): keep your ass toned

BBG (6/18/2009 11:51:33 AM): oh lol I always dance

BBG (6/18/2009 11:51:39 AM): yes it's toned

Roe grand (6/18/2009 11:51:48 AM): where have you been dancing?

BBG (6/18/2009 11:51:58 AM): at home lol

He would travel back and forth from London to Amsterdam to visit with his family. Four days after he had made such a trip, he contacted me. I had just told him I had returned from attending a friend's birthday party. As was usual, he always found a way to turn the conversation to sex. He began to ask me how many people attended the party, if they were all gay, if they were Nigerian's and how many of them were sexy. My reply was innocent as I told him I wasn't paying attention to any of them so I didn't know. I told him they were all good friends I had gotten to know when I moved to Chicago and that not for a second did I ever think of any of them in a sexual manner. I thought that would have settled his curiosity, but instead it only piqued it. He went on and asked how many of them were tops and bottoms, which instantly irritated me. He must have noticed my mood change as I was replying slower and with single word responses. He once told me I was beautiful and I would be perfect as an escort I could make tons of money. These were the types of conversations he enjoyed. Vie said he wouldn't care what I did for a living so long as I was doing my services in front of him.

It was depressing knowing that the only reason someone wanted to speak to me was because it was about sex.

Roe grand (6/24/2009 1:27:40 PM): hi Tunde

BBG (6/24/2009 1:28:26 PM): hey

Roe grand (6/24/2009 1:28:37 PM): how are you today

BBG (6/24/2009 1:31:20 PM): not so good

Roe grand (6/24/2009 1:31:29 PM): oh why?

BBG (6/24/2009 1:31:53 PM): I'm just sad vie I'm lonely

Roe grand (6/24/2009 1:32:07 PM): you got lots of friends

BBG (6/24/2009 1:33:15 PM): not really

Roe grand (6/24/2009 1:40:10 PM): ok so u got a sexy story for me

*Roe grand (6/24/2009 1:40:33 PM): let's pretend I'm just coming home and find u there naked_*

There was no use trying, Vie was one of those guys that was focused on their own interests. I was sure he would find someone who would feed all of his online sexual fantasies even if at that time I didn't think I was that person.

15

Vie loved his sexual bedtime stories and never went offline without them. At this point, I knew he was full of it, but I kept on talking to him hoping that I might change his ways. He told me once that he wanted to propose to me though he had never met me in person. I clung to that thought and foolishly started feeling on top of the world. When I asked him if he had someone he is seeing in addition to me he said not really. For normal people that usually a yes or no question. One day Vie floored me by asking if I would come to London to visit him. I had long ago chalked him up to a flirt which would go no further than online chat and the occasional phone call when one of us decided to incur the cost. Of course there was a catch to it. Vie said he would only pay for me to come and see him in London if I would agree to have sex with him the entire time without a condom. I wasn't surprised he threatened to not send a ticket if I didn't agree of letting him have his way. So, just to please him I agreed to not use a condom so he could at least buy the ticket for me to come to Europe. The closer the time got for me to go, the more apprehensive I because about the situation. So instead I made a backup plan in case things didn't go well with Vie while I was in London.

My idea for wanting to get out of town was twofold. I did want to finally meet Vie in person, but I also needed to get out of town for a mental vacation to at least escape the sadness that was slowly starting to catch up to me.

I had a friend from high school in Nigeria that lived in London. My friend Kolawole Adewuyi was a fellow gay friend who made it clear to any and all who knew him that he would only date white men who of course would have to be financially stable for him. Even though I had not seen him since leaving Nigeria we had remained in contact on my messenger whenever I was online.

It was Kolawole and not Vie who immediately booked the very next flight for me after I had told him I was planning to come to London. Vie managed to conveniently disappear a week before I was to leave Chicago and never did contact me while I was in London or when I finally returned. Instead my friend he even surprised me with a first class ticket. He called as I was reading the email flight confirmation for my trip.

"Hey Ashawo (Yoruba word for prostitute)," he greeted excitedly as I answered my cell phone.

"Don't call me that I have changed my ways," I said smiling to myself.

"Oh whatever bitch, you know you love dick and can't let it go."

You love it in the day, afternoon, night, all month and all year round," he added.

"Please stop this harassment," I teased, laughing.

"Whatever, who is harassing you? I am calling about all the wonderful boys I have here for you in London," he said.

"Oh really?" I asked, now focusing more on my conversation with him and less on the details of my flight.

"Yes really, and I'm thinking we can take the train to Paris to catch a friends party, you need to meet him too when you get here."

"I don't know about all that, I'm on a budget," I said.

"Bitch I hope you are not gonna come all the way here and be laying on the coach and be watching TV the whole time!" he yelled. I could tell his hands were on his hips when he said it.

"Didn't I tell you if you don't have money my husband will handle the bills while you are here?"

"Thank you so much for everything," I said genuinely, I didn't know how I would be able to repay his generosity.

"Oh hun anytime you're so welcome," he said.

"Actually, I should be saying thanks to your husband, is he there?" I asked.

"No, he is not but someone else is," he supplied.

"Are you kidding me?" I asked incredulously.

"What you mean," he asked innocently.

"You are joking that someone else is there right?" I asked.

"It's not what you think," he replied.

"I hope it's not I mean you have a good one don't mess it up," I said, feeling a little pang on jealously at my friends relationship.

"Of course not it's just my designer sketching things up for my next show," he said. Kolawole was a designer with an independent boutique which seemed to be doing quite well from what he shared about his business.

"Hmmm if you say so," I said skeptically.

"Oh bitch get off the phone," he finished. Don't forget to text me the time you will be arriving and all that info," he added before signing off.

"Ok I will," I answered before hanging up.

The flight to London was one of the best flights I had ever taken because I was riding first class. The seating was spacious and it felt as if even the flight attendants were nicer in first class.

On arriving at the Heathrow Airport I was very excited to see my friend Kolawole who was already there waiting for me to arrive. That first night, we talked all night about everything that had been going on with each of us since we had left Nigeria. He shared with me that he was finally planning his dream wedding with his husband. Kolawole asked if I could perform a dance at his wedding as part of the entertainment during the reception.

I was starting to feel a little bit of peace at last from the environment I had left in Chicago. I allowed myself to sit back and think about what it was I had been doing to find love and not allowing it to find me. Kolwaole assured me that the men in London were totally different than the ones I had left behind in the US. In fact, there were a lot of Nigerian gay men in London, and there was even a little community which they had carved out for themselves I was told. I thought it wouldn't hurt to try my search for love while in

London since I was in a different environment. My friend suggested a popular nightspot which was located near a shopping mall.

Kolawole and I planned to attend together that first Friday that I was in London. He said he would make sure and get off of work a little early so we could enjoy a nice dinner beforehand prior to heading to the club. He had called up one of his friends by the name of Jamar to join us for the evening. He was hoping that the two of us would make a connection once we had met. After telling me about Jamar, I was hopeful as well, he sounded rather handsome and seemed like a sweet person from Kolawole description.

As Friday approached I was growing more excited about our first official outing. I had already spoken one on the phone with Jamar and he seemed just as excited about meeting me as well. By midday I had already decided to feed into my own curiosity about Jamar and I took him up on his invitation to meet up with him prior to dinner with Kolawole.

At around 4pm, I headed out. I met Jamar that day at the intersection of Regent St. and Oxford, where we had agreed upon. He stood 6' tall had a football players build that was neither fat nor muscular but definitely defined from head to toe. He had a caramel complexion with brownish hair and eyes. When he greeted me was the first time that I noticed a West Indian accent. When we had spoken on the phone, I took for granted that it was simply an African accent without having asked. But in person I could tell from the way he emphasized certain words that it was not so much African as it was West Indian.

He explained that he had just moved from Jamaica to live in

London. It was understood that we were both from countries where homosexuality was considered a crime. We had decided earlier to do some window shopping at the strip mall area near the club while we waited for Kolawole to arrive. So, we talked from one thing to the next while he led the way and showed me around. Each time he walked forward he had to turn to look back to see if I was keeping up with him. I was smaller than him and I was trying to keep up with his long strides.

Around 6pm, Kolawole called to see where we were so that he could meet up with us. I could tell from the sound of his voice, he was not happy about the fact that I had changed the plans and came out to meet Jamar on my own.

"So what happened to the plan Ashawo?" he asked, but I could tell he wasn't joking when he called me it this time.

"I figured it couldn't hurt to come and hang out," I said.

"But you don't even know this guy," he said.

I put my finger up as I was talking to indicate to Jamar that I would only be on the phone briefly. I stepped further away so that I could have some privacy, because I didn't want him to know that my friend was annoyed about my decision to stray from the plan.

"Well we have been talking on the phone," I whispered.

"What's the problem are you upset because he is one of your little side projects?" I added in smartly.

"Bitch, you don't know this guy, I was going to do proper introductions and give you a little more insight on how to handle this guy," he said.

I didn't know what he meant by handling him, but by that time I was annoyed as well.

"Perhaps, tonight is not a good night to hang out," I said.

"Whatever, you need to listen and not act on your first thought all the time," he continued scolding.

"Fine, I am going to be heading back, I don't want to go out tonight," I ended hanging up before he could issue another reprimand.

When I walked by over to Jamar, I could tell that he must have picked up at least every other word of my conversation as it started to get a little heated. The look on his face was one of concerned and curiosity.

"Everything is fine," I said, stopping him from asking any questions.

"But I think it might be best if I just went back to Kolawole's house instead," I suggested.

"Why?" asked Jamar. "We were getting along fine, weren't we?"

"Yes, it's not that, but I have to respect his wishes, he is the one responsible for bringing me out here." I explained.

"Hmm… and what if I won't let you go?" he asked smiling.

"Well…then I would have an excuse for staying," I said.

In answer he grabbed by hand and led me further along the walk, heading to the other side of the strip mall. Kolawole called two other times, but must have given up when I didn't answer the second time. As the day started to get darker we decided to stop at his place before heading the club, he said he wanted me to check out one his movies. He claimed to be a popular actor in Jamaica and I had simply laughed about it because I thought he was just joking around. He seemed offended and to prove himself he pulled out his phone and entered his name on the search screen. To my surprise his face did pop up as a popular actor out of Jamaica and there were films listed under his name.

Since he said he wanted to continue showing me various parts of London, we decided to take one of the city buses to his home instead of driving. We left his car parked at the mall and grabbed a bus, which made sense to me since we were going to be going to the club that night anyway.

The ride to his home took about an hour and half from the location where we were. When we excited the bus at his top, his whole demeanor changed. I couldn't quite put my finger on it, but he seemed a little more distant physically, like someone who had just happened to get off on the same stop with someone else and not like two people who were traveling purposefully together.

Suddenly he looked back at me and said, "Why are you walking like that?"

"What do you mean?" I asked.

"Why you walking like that?" he asked again.

"What do you mean?" I returned more emphatically, and totally confused.

"You are not walking right," he said.

"I don't understand," I returned.

"Man you are switching like a girl," he said.

"Well this is how I walk, I was walking like this before we got here," I said, now regretting my decision to come with him to home.

"So you walk like a bitch, only bitches walk like that man, walk the right way," he urged.

I couldn't figure out why all of a sudden walking mattered when we had been hanging out for the past few hours. A part of me was screaming in my head back to go back to the bus stop and wait for the next one to take me back. It would have been easy enough to retrace my steps and head back in the other direction.

In the back and forth about my walk, we had reached what was apparently the front of his flat.

"Wait here man I'll let you know when to come in," he said.

"Uh, ok," I replied.

This would have been the perfect opportunity for me to run, but sometimes we don't ever listen to that inner voice of warning.

It took about ten minutes for him to do whatever it was he needed to do on the inside of his flat, he opened the door slightly and poked his head out to give me a signal that it was ok to enter.

When I walked in he said, "Well this is my house do you like it?"

"Yes, it looks nice," I said.

"Do you live alone?" I asked. I had visions of him hiding away a wife while I stood outside waiting.

"Yes I do," he said. "Do you want something to drink?"

"No I'm ok and I can't stay for long anyway," I added. I think Kolawole is going to be waiting at the club for me even though we had it out on the phone," I said giving myself an excuse to leave early.

"But I thought we were gonna watch one of my movies together?"

"I didn't forget but my friend wants me back home earlier," I said nervously, confusing the lie.

"As a matter of fact, I told him I was going to be on my way back to his house already," I said.

"Well before you leave then can I get a hug?" he asked, outstretching his arms.

"Sure I guess," I said walking slowly towards him.

As I walked closer to allow him to hug me, he closed the gap between us quickly and gripped me tightly in a bear hug restraining my arms from in turn encircling him. It seemed like we stood in that position for a good minute before I started to try and pull back. It seemed as though he was going to allow me to end the hug, but instead he moved in and kissed me without ceremony. Within a few seconds it turned from a mild kiss to an aggressive one when I started to try to pull away. Simultaneously he grabbed my ass which further prevented me from pulling away. I managed to place my hands on his chest to give myself some leverage in being able to pull away, but I could barely breath he was holding me so tightly against him.

"Wait a minute, take it easy," I managed to get out.

"You know you want to fuck me," he said in response.

I was too confused about what was about to happen, I felt as though I couldn't gather my thoughts about what my next move should be, which in the end put him at an advantage. His place was dim and I couldn't see where he was dragging me to until I felt the bed break my fall when he pushed me down.

"Please, can you at least turn on the light so I can see?" I pleaded. But my request was met with the sound of him unbuckling his pants. I could hear as they dropped to the floor. I couldn't make out anything, by now the minimal light that had been streaming through the windows had all but disappeared. In a flash he was kneeling over me, I could feel the bed depress as he placed either knee next to my face.

I could hear myself let out a scream, which didn't last long as he shoved his dick in my mouth and proceeded to choke me.

My mouth couldn't even take it all even though I tried to relax so I wouldn't gag.

"Suck it bitch," he said gruffly above me in the dark.

I did as I was instructed, I was too scared not to, so I sucked him so slowly trying not to make him angry. I figured if I did this he would let me go afterwards. I could feel him starting to pump harder in my mouth, but before he could come, he pulled out and turned me over roughly on the bed. He was still straddling me and I couldn't pull my arms up from under the weight of his body. I didn't dare fight, he was much bigger than me and I would have lost the fight anyway. So I complied with everything he told me to do.

"Assume the fucking position," he ordered.

"Ok, ok…do you have a condom?" I asked meekly.

"Yeah I do," he responded.

But before I could realize it, he rammed his dick in me, before I could even prepare myself for the onslaught.

"Where is the condom?" I asked which was muffled because he had placed his hand on the back on my head forcing my face into the bed.

"Man hold the fuck on I'm just testing my dick," he said.

"Please, please, put on a condom," I begged.

"Shut the fuck up man I ain't gonna fuck you without a condom cool down," he yelled.

"Ok man just let me suck you off instead of getting fucked," I suggested.   Momentarily, my suggestion must have sounded like a more attractive option, because I was back on my back and his dick was back in my mouth.

"I still wanna fuck that round big ass," he said to me, his voice now sounded as though he was about to come. He won't be able to I thought to myself if he comes, he will be ready to pass out I hoped.

Once again he stopped himself and got off me in a rushed manner. The look on his face was one of anger and disgust. I couldn't figure out what was going on, I just wanted him to be done. He grabbed me off the bed only to slap me across my face. The blow was so hard that I flew to the floor in a daze.

As I was trying to pull myself up from the floor he climbed on me once again turning me over so that I was face down on the floor. By now I had started to struggle to get from under his weight. I was frightened, I knew now that he was not going to happy with just getting his dick sucked. He was not going to let me leave his place without doing more damage.

As I struggled under him he head butted me immediately made me see stars in the darkness. By then he had forced himself in me once again. I started to scream, but it was met with a head shove to the floor. I could taste the blood starting to pool in my mouth as I lay there with him on top of me.

"Shut the fuck up and take it like a fag you fucking bitch!"

As painful as it was he forced every inch of himself in me. It felt as though he had ripped me open. I had never felt pain like that before while ever having sex.

The painful part of being raped by Jamar was that it wasn't quick instead Jamar took his time which made it feel like forever.

I was afraid of being killed; I had no other choice than to let him do what he wanted. He never did get that condom instead, he further disgraced me and stood up from me when it was over and ejaculated all over my face. I put up my arms to protect myself, but he pulled them away from my face as I cried in pain.

I laid there helpless wondering what would happen next, when I felt the weight of a big object, it must have been a chair that hit me square on my chest. I couldn't breathe and I struggled to gasp for air.

For a moment I thought I had died when I couldn't catch my breath, until I heard him yell, "Get the fuck out of my house you fucking faggot ass bitch!" in his thick accent.

I leaped up pulling up my pants as I frantically moved towards the door. I didn't know whether he was directly behind me or if he hadn't moved at all, I just knew I had to get out of there. Before I could reach the doorknob, I felt the blow of a stick on the back of my neck.

"Please just let me go," I begged.

When I turned, I saw it was a broom he had in his hand. He lifted it again, bringing it down on my face and head with the second blow. He beat me there right in the foyer of his flat. As he was beating me, I remembered the first beating I had ever received at the hands of someone I had sex with, it made me cry even harder. When I got out, I was lying face down on the corner of his block. I could barely see out of one eye. But I managed to find my cell phone which was under me to dial Kolawole's number to come and help me. After I hung up the phone, I put my head back on the concrete and simply prayed.

As soon as Kolawole came to the scene he started to scream from the shock of seeing me bathed in blood and beaten up. He immediately grabbed me off of the sidewalk and lifted me into the back seat of his car to lie down.

"Where is that bastard?!!"

"Please just get me out of here," I said in a weak tone.

"Are you crazy? How can we leave and let him get away with this?"

"Let's go, please, Kolawole, please," I begged, I just wanted to get out of there.

"If he thinks Jamaicans are crazy, he's never seen crazy until I show him what a Naija person can do!" he yelled.

"Please, I don't know where he is, I don't want to get hurt again," I cried.

Kolawole then got into the driver seat and started speeding to get through the traffic. I thought he was taking me to a hospital at first until I could see his building coming into view through my blurred vision. When he had gotten me into his place, he grabbed towel from the guest bathroom room which was located to the right as soon as you entered the flat.

He cleaned up the blood which had started to dry on my face and then dialed the police. While we waited for them to arrive, Kolawole started pacing back and forth in anger and suggesting he could pay people to go to Jamar's house and beat him up severely in return for what he had done to me.

When the policed finally arrived, they questioned me about how and where I had met Jamar, his description and what exactly had happened. While I was telling the officers what happened they took photos of my arms and face noting my bruises. They took down the approximate location of the house and asked if I wanted to press charges.

Before I could answer Kolawole screamed, "Yes!"

Both officers turned to him, telling him it was a question that was meant for me to answer. I immediately agreed as I saw the look on Kolawole's face waiting for me to say 'yes'.

They told me they would check the location of the scene and from the description I had given them. As soon as they left Kolawole told me that I should be rest assured because the police in London were quick to respond to American citizens who were visiting and became victims of crime.

The next day while Kolawole was at work, I called the police department and dropped the charges. I was scared and I blamed myself for the predicament that I had gotten myself into. I never told him what I had done. By the time I left London, I told him perhaps they were still in the midst of their investigation and hadn't caught up to Jamar yet. I told him to contact me if he heard anything more about the case.

I never did hear from Vie that entire time in London. I wasn't sure I would have been any better off had I did hear from him. What started off as an adventure ended up being my biggest nightmare.

16

When I got back from London, I began concentrating more on school and the important things in my life. I was starting to think about my life more deeply at this point and was starting to realize all of the things I may have been doing wrong and why I was still in the end single. I knew I needed some mental healing with all that had gone on, but I wasn't quite sure where I needed to start.

It annoyed me when I would share my story with others only to have people tell me, "Why worry, you're young have your fun!"

One day on campus, I met up with one of my first roommates. Josiah was straight, but he was always nice to me and didn't care about me being gay.

I remember one day he asked "Tunde how do you know if your gay if you haven't tried having pussy?"

And I had responded, "Well how are you totally sure you are straight if you have not messed with a guy?"

When we lived together he would always come to me whenever he needed advice about certain things in his relationship that he couldn't figure out for himself. It's odd how I couldn't figure out my own relationship problems but I was always able to give him helpful advice at least as far as he was concerned. I shared with Josiah about some of the things that had occurred with me and he was kind and showed concern. He suggested I join a support center which was located over in the gay area of Chicago. I had been by that location tons of times, but I never knew what it was they did or offered by way of services.

That day when I entered the doors of the center I felt at home, there were individuals of different races, shapes and sizes. I took a tour of the building by myself that first day. There were three floors; the first floor had a large reception desk with an open seating area that lead to a café which adjoined the center. On the second floor there was a huge computer room where you could sign up for free usage. At the time there were people ranging in age from 13 to adults using the computers.

I looked towards my right when I stepped out of the computer room and saw a long striped hallway and on the walls were pictures of famous events that involved the GLBT community. A door opened towards the end of the hall and, out came a team of basket ball players all still amped up from their game. There were stairs just past the gym which lead up to the third floor. There were closed doors all along the hall which held signs stating the various classes that were in session. I stopped at the one which announced a dance class was being held inside. As I was looking through the view window located on the door and concentrating on one of the dance classes, I heard from behind me over my shoulder, "I've never seen you here before, what's your name?"

"My name is Tunde" I replied simultaneously turning around to see who was making the inquiry.

"What is your name?" I asked.

Before he could in turn reply with his name someone came towards us saying.

"His name is Rob and he is a whore so he is only talking to you to get in your pants next."

"Yeah you're next on the list," another person came forward to say right beside us.

I replied saying, "Wow your quite popular Rob."

As we were talking a girl joined and started saying, "Do y'all know they caught Marcus fucking in the bathroom?"

One of the boy's replied, "Shit he's been on everyone's dick except for you honey." pointing in my direction.

Then he asked "Are you a bottom or top?"

I was a bit puzzled and didn't feel comfortable answering that question, luckily that's when Rob saved me, "It ain't anyone's business what he is." Then we all laughed together, in unison like a choir.

"Girl he has slept with Maury and Maury's father," one of the boys continued.

"Like real father or play father?" I asked.

"Real father like blood father," one of my new gossiping friends answered.

One of the Staff came up on the floor through the same doorway I entered and announced aloud "It's time for groups!"

I could tell it was an important announcement, because everyone who had gathered in the hall with me suddenly began making their way to one of the doors along the hall which had a sign up that said, Open Discussion Group on the door.

That first day, I simply listened. People spoke about what it was like for them to be gay, what had happened to them when they came out, and what they wanted for their lives beyond what they currently had. It was nice not to have to say anything especially since it was my first time, I wasn't sure I knew exactly what I would have shared anyway.

I even saw a friend from the clubs at the group. Gary wasn't a close friend, but whenever I saw him at the club, he always had this million dollar smile on his face like he had just won the lottery. After the group, we sat on the stairs on the first floor and talked. We parted ways in front of the center and I stood there watching him leave, I felt good about coming to the center. I would have to thank Josiah for suggesting it to me.

17

That night, as I made my way home, I ran through all the things I had been through. I wasn't sure if I would ever get up in the group and share all of it, but maybe certain parts. I saw that there was no judgment as people were sharing. And even the gossipy ones that I had met in front of the group that night, were all respectful and listened quietly as people shared in the group.

I was deep in my thoughts as I reached my block. I didn't even see the familiar face that was leaning against his car as I approached my building.

It was Leo. Leo and I hadn't talked that much since me and Aaron had hit it off that night at his apartment.

"Hi there," I said as I walked toward him.

"How are you Tunde?" asked Leo.

"I'm fine, what are you doing here?" I asked.

"You ran through my thoughts and I wanted to see if maybe I could catch up to you," he answered.

"Thanks?" I said still surprised by the unannounced visit. I wasn't sure if I wanted him to come upstairs into my apartment so I leaned next to him against his car to see how the conversation would go.

We made the usual small talk of people who hadn't seen each other in awhile.

"I met a new boy," said Leo.

"Really, are you serious?" I asked.

"Yes and he is from Nigeria," continued Leo.

He then said he had also met him on Adam 4 Steve and that he would introduce me to him when he saw me next.

Leo asked if I had eaten dinner yet, I was almost glad that he asked that instead of if he could come up to my place. I hadn't eaten so we decided to go around the corner to the diner which had pretty good burger.

We sat and made light conversation until our food came out. I was surprised Leo seemed concerned about how I was doing physically and asked if I made it a point to use condoms. We were at the restaurant until about 1am before we headed back to my apartment so Leo could drop me off. As we were driving we passed some young men who were obviously working

Why aren't they at home and where are their parents?" I asked to no one in particular.

"Parents?" repeated Leo.

"Their parents really don't care about them, so to survive they have to sell the next best thing, themselves. Many are thrown out of their houses because of their sexuality and as you can see many of them are also black."

"Yeah I see," I responded.

"Its trouble to be gay but its double trouble to be black and gay," he continued.

We were stopped at a red light and several cars in front of us; we saw what looked like a male in drag entering a car. Once we had reached to my place, I thanked Leo, told him I would give him a call and headed upstairs. I was tired, I had seen and heard a lot for the day and I wanted to just replay things and put everything in perspective.

Over the next few weeks Leo and I talked over the phone quite a bit. Although he did try to ask me out again on a date, I turned him down, I was enjoying relating to him as a potential friend. It was with Leo that I experienced going to my first bathhouse. It was located at this placed called Hot Works which was in Boys Village. I didn't quite know what it was only that you could get massages and soak in the hot tub. There was membership fee which was $25 and in addition you had to pay for a locker if you needed it.

When you entered after paying you were given a plain white towel at the front desk. Leo explained that there were certain unspoken codes about how you carried yourself once you were inside.

"If you are holding your locker key in your left hand, you are a bottom."

"In your right hand, and you are a top."

"Ok," I whispered behind him.

"Why don't you go get undressed and meet me at the showers," he said.

"Ok," I said, heading towards one of the bathroom stalls to get undressed. When I came out I didn't see Leo, so I headed over to lock my clothes into my assigned locker. I only had on the towel around my waist at this point and nothing else.

After I locked up my clothes I headed around the corner to where the showers were which we had passed on our way in. The shower was out in the open in a corner of a large room which also had open seating in the center of the room. Across the hall from the showers there was gym with glass surrounding it. While I showered I hung my towel in front of me on the waist high towel bar so I wouldn't feel as thought I was giving the boys in the gym area a show.

Once I was done showering I wrapped my towel around me and headed for the stairs since I didn't see Leo yet. As I headed to towards the stairs I had to pass several men who were standing along the hallway leading to the stairs. A couple of them reached out and stroked my chest as I walked by, I didn't know it was normal or ok for the men to touch a person walking by without asking or introducing themselves. Along the stairwell there were men kissing as they unwrapped their towels. I didn't have time to stay and watch because I in search of Leo just then. When I had reached the second floor, along this hallway was what Leo referred to as glory holes. Men would bend down waiting for a guy on the other side of the wall to stick their penis in the hole and would then proceed to give them an anonymous blow job. All throughout the place, I noticed there were what I called cheerleaders. Guys who were simply encouraging all that was going on.

"Yeah fuck his brains out," was a highly common cheer.

I wasn't really feeling the scene just yet, so I decided to go back downstairs to the open pool area that was located on the other side of the gym and simply wait for Leo to make reappearance.

I got in the pool and the water felt warm and that relaxed me despite the busy scene around me. It was now going on about three hours since we had here when Leo finally came walking towards me looking frustrated and upset.

"Let's go to Boy's country," he said pouting a little.

"Boy's country what's that?" I asked.

"It's like this place but cheaper and a lot of more black guys go there."

So in about thirty minutes, we were on our way to Boy's Country. By now it was around 2 or 3am.

Once we had parked Leo grabbed what he called his kit pack which I have come to know contains his condoms, lube and gloves. We checked in at the front desk and paid our ten dollars to get in. He was right there were lots more black men at this location than the last, which was nice.

We ended the night after a few hours. We ended up leaving around 7:00am. I was worn out from standing and walk around at both locations. When Leo dropped me off at my apartment, I barely remembered getting upstairs and into bed. I didn't wake up later on until noon.

18

For the remainder of the month I tried living in the real world for a change. I was determined to wean myself off the gay internet world and just live. One of the things I started to cultivate was my dancing. I began auditioning at local shows that were being held in the Chicago area. The worse that could happen was I would get a no, but at least it took my focus off of the internet.

I also started taking voice lessons. My boss even noted that I seemed more focused at work and had improved on my attendance record.

Through one of my auditions, I managed to get a gig performing in drag and it turned out to be a huge success. During one performance I was featured in one of the local Chicago newspapers.

During this time, I started thinking about my mother back in Nigeria. With all that had been going on I never told her about my gay life because it was forbidden back home to be gay. So I always kept things surface and in general during our conversations. I knew that one day I would tell her, when that day would be was the big question.

Leo even came out to support during my drag show. He finally introduced me to his new boy toy, Sammy. Before he brought Sammy to meet me, I felt nervous that it might be someone I knew back in Nigeria. I did not want my business getting back to my family before I had a chance to tell them myself.

When Leo introduced us, the first thing he asked was if I could still speak our native language. I said that yes, I could, and he commenced to speaking to me. He complimented me on my performance and said he didn't know of any other Nigerian drag performer bold enough to perform out in public. He asked why I used my real name for my performances instead of a made up name like the other performers. But I always felt, since my name was different anyway, why bother changing it. The conversation then turned to Sammy asking me where I stayed in Nigeria. As soon as I told him he asked me if I knew a girl by the name of Kisata.

"Yes, that's my cousin," I replied.

Sammy knew my cousin from high school. They had attended high school together before she had passed away.

"What a small world," I said aloud.

Leo then told us to speak English. We both laughed, since we knew it was killing him to know what it was we were saying to one another.

Over the next few weeks that passed I got to be great friends with Sammy, more like brothers actually. He introduced me to another gay Nigerian but he was an older gentleman that later became more of a father figure for me than my own Dad.

19

After about two to three months of my hiatus, I went back to the gay scene hungry for love and for some attention.

I found him under the featured sexiest listing on Black Gay Convo. I viewed his page and his pictures took my breath away. Immediately I emailed him and told him I wouldn't mind getting to know him. Luckily for me he was online and he replied right back asking if I had read his profile because he was in North Carolina and not in Chicago.

I responded that I only wanted a chat buddy. It took a while for us to finally talk on the phone because he kept saying that he had been physically abused by his ex and was nervous about his ex setting some sort of trap for him by impersonating someone on the computer. I let him know that I wanted to be friends and get to know him but that I would never hurt him. I also shared with him that I had been down that road as well so I knew how it felt.

He became more comfortable and ended up giving me his number. Usually when someone gave me their number, I called right away. But Sammy was always being big brother and told me to stop being so eager when meeting someone new. After about two days I called him while I was in school during a break in my day.

He couldn't pronounce my name even with me saying it slowly and trying to coach him through it, so we agreed that he would call me 'Tee' for short instead. His name was Tavin Mackey.

Tavin and I talked for about 3 hours that first day. We seemed to have quite a bit in common, mostly our bad luck as of late in men and some instances of abuse within past encounters with men. I wasn't sure if this similarity was a good or a bad thing, but it felt good to talk about it all with him. And it seemed as though he was beginning to trust me enough to share his story with me.

About a month into our chats, Tavin said he was coming to the Chicago area to visit a friend and thought that maybe he could seize the opportunity to meet me while he was up this way.

He said he had been in Chicago once before but only for a short while. I asked him how long he was going to be staying and he said about a month.

I agreed that it would be nice to finally meet in person and told him to give me a call when he was in Chicago and we could meet for lunch or dinner.

The day came before he was to arrive and I was nervous about meeting him. So I called my friend Sammy and talked to him about Tavin. Sammy told me to just be myself.

The day he called me to meet him, he had already been in Chicago for a few days. We decided to go and have lunch around downtown Chicago at a popular pizza place. On my way to the destination I called Sammy so he could give me some confidence to alleviate my jitters.

"Would you cool down?" Sammy said. "Just be yourself when you meet him like I told you before," he continued.

"Maybe I should cover my braids it might be too feminine for him," I said.

"You must be crazy then, why would you change yourself for someone that you might not see again?" Sammy asked.

"Good question," I replied.

"That's what brothers are for, just let me know how it goes," Sammy ended as he hung up. I had hung up just in time because I was walking up on our meeting place. I knew who he was the instant I saw him, his description of himself was the most accurate I had ever received. He was leaning against the parking meter looking directly at me. I guess I hadn't done a bad job of describing myself either.

"Hi Tavin," I said shyly walking towards him.

"Hi Tee," he replied.

"How are you?" I asked.

"I am fine, but I will be better once I get a hug," he flirted.

I came closer and gave him a hug and whispered, "I am glad you decided to meet me."

"Me too," he whispered back.

"So what do you have planned today?" I asked.

"I thought maybe we could get a bite to eat and then see a movie," he replied.

"That sounds good to me," I said.

"Is pizza ok or did you have something different in mind?" he asked.

"Well you are the visitor, plus you can't leave without having sampled some of our famous Chicago style pizza," I added.

Lunch was great, we talked about where he was from and he in turn asked me questions about Nigeria. I always liked talking about Nigeria because it made me feel as though I was back at home again. I don't remember what movie we ended up going to see, because we talked throughout the movie from one thing to the next. He was a perfect gentleman during the movie and only asked for a kiss at the end of the day after we had hung out. He was not aggressive or rude and it was a great change from what I had been allowing myself to experience. Since Tavin had a few more weeks to spend in Chicago before he was to leave we agreed that we would hang out a few more times before he left. But after the second week, Tavin became ill due to the cold Chicago winter weather. He became so ill, that he had to check into the county hospital. The day I went to see him at the hospital I cancelled my classes and called in sick to work so I could spend the majority of my day with him.

On my way to the hospital, I got him some food since he kept complaining about the taste of the hospital meals.

By the time I reached his room there was a nurse standing out front of his door. She greeted me and handed me a face mask that would cover my nose and mouth. I was wondering what exactly had happened to Tavin that would require me to wear a mask.

In the room there was another nurse that sat right beside Tavin. Tavin looked very ill as he lay in the bed; it was my first time seeing his bare chest since we had been seeing each other. When he saw me his face lit up and he began struggling to sit up as I walked further in the room.

Laughing he said, "Damn they got you wearing this mask stuff, shit it's not that serious."

"I know right," I said and laughed as well.

I passed his food over to him and he said, "Aww you're so sweet, I'm so lucky to be with you."

I sat next to him as he opened up the to-go carton of food I had brought and watched him eat. I told him about how my morning had gone before coming to see him as he ate.

After a few minutes had passed once he had finished his food and the nurse had excused herself. He reached over to grab my hand.

"I have something to tell you," he said.

"Ok, I'm listening," I said.

"Well for a while now I have been thinking how I was going to tell you this, but the thing is I really like you and I'm not sure if I can give you all the love you're looking for right now," he said. "What I really mean is your so young and I keep thinking you haven't been out there, how are you even sure you want me in my condition."

"I'm young but I know what I want, I have been looking for someone that is open to all that I am and that's you," I said interrupting him.

"You're going to be healthy in a few days," I said wondering what the purpose of the big speech was.

"Tunde the thing is I am HIV positive and I don't think it's fair to you to be with me."

I was surprised by this admission, but not scared. HIV and AIDS were not diseases I had not heard about.

"I don't care what you have that's what condoms are for, I'm willing to make this work, all my life I've been looking for someone real, that can accept me for who I really am and all that I am."

As I looked at him, I could see his eyes starting to well up, just as mine were. He reached over, removed my mask and gave me a light peck on my lips.

We didn't really talk about anything after that. I was letting the weight of his information settle with me and I think he was allowing that to happen and just lay there quietly. I stayed until visiting hours were over and then headed home.

As soon as I got home I called Sammy and told him my situation with Tavin. Once I had mentioned he was HIV positive Sammy seemed a bit freaked out about it and questioned if I really knew what I was getting myself into and if we had already had sex. One thing Sammy was clear about was that it was really my decision and he would support me no matter what.

The next time I went to see him he talked to me about his friend James who he had originally came to visit. He was a teacher with the Chicago public school system and they had met online years before, but had remained friends. I shared with Tavin about my friends and we compared who had the crazier brood.

Tavin was in the hospital for about a week overall. Little by little Tavin started disclosing about his current situation. He had been living on unemployment because ever since he became sick it was affecting his attendance and ability to do his work. So his employers had agreed to lay him off so that he could collect unemployment. He had come to stay with James indefinitely to see if being in Chicago would be a better fit for him financially.

The following week that he was out of the hospital he began interviewing for a free live in facility which catered to HIV/AIDs positive individuals. By staying there he would be able to save up the money he was getting from unemployment and get himself financially stable once again.

While he was getting himself settled, I continued to support in whatever way I could. One morning I opened my mail and saw that he had sent me a letter. It read:

Tunde,

To help you start your day I thought I would write you a letter. When I go to this place baby I don't know what it holds or what it's about. I just feel I must deal with it, because after being in Chicago I can now see I eventually need to get my own place because how else can I spend all the time I want with you. I feel something special in my heart for you and this feeling has only happened once to me (the one time I knew I was in love) but I know it's so soon so I guess we will see. Did you know every time I see you no matter how bad I feel I'm so happy? I feel I have a best friend when I'm with you. You know I love your voice, the way your body moves, your spirit, your hair. Well I guess I'm saying you're perfect for me.

Now let's talk serious, I'm in the middle of some changes that are going to be rough for me, and I just can't be in a relationship but I can't lose you Tunde so I'm willing to try and see where it goes. I see myself happy with you, but understand why it scares me. I've been hurt and used so much I never thought I could do it again. If you feel you may be able to hurt me Tunde tell me now and end it. I don't want to be the boy you're having fun with for the moment. If we try this relationship it may not be easy at first but I promise to give my all, and be there for you, to be your rock and be your man. I will never allow another to come between that. Of course we need to talk more and I need know how you feel, but take your time I want you to be sure.

I love you Tunde I really do and I knew it from the second time you visited me in the hospital. I was sure of it then, it meant the world to me.

Tavin

That weekend I decided to take him with me to Sammy's place to spend the weekend with me. It was a traditional way for Nigerians to let their close relatives know that they have found the one. Tavin came to get me at home and we both rode the train to Sammy's place. Sammy opened the door for us and said, "Where is your husband to be?" in a joking manner.

I responded in Nigerian Pidgin English to him saying, "U de craze abeg leave me alone." (You're crazy)

"He is locking the car and bringing the last bag with him," I said.

When Tavin walked in, Sammy gave him a hug and welcomed him in Yoruba. I was pleased that even though Sammy was not 100% for the relationship out of concern for me, he was putting his best foot forward.

John came over as well to join in the festivities.

Sammy and John had decided that they would prepare a traditional Nigerian meal for Tavin to try. They had made, Iyan (pounded yams), Obe Efo (vegetable soup), and stewed chicken. As is typical for many African countries, we used our hands to eat, but I made sure Tavin had a fork just in case. We all laughed when he dropped his fork and commenced eating his food in the same manner that we were, with his fingers.

To break the silence during out dinner, John started talking about politics, current affairs and sports. None of which peaked the interest of myself or Sammy. The only thing Sammy and I could add to the topics was which player or political figure was handsome or well dressed. Then the topic switched to who the ideal guy would be to date in a perfect situation.

"I would rather deal with a married guy that way I would be competing against a woman instead of another guy," said Sammy.

Tavin replied, "That is totally wrong you're breaking up happy homes."

"Happy homes?" said Sammy.

"If they were happy they wouldn't be coming to us gay boys to do them right!"

John then joined in and said, "Hmm... their dick in one hand and the wedding ring in the other, I mean these guys are confused, you can't be bisexual choose one."

"Well they were forced into stuff and now it's too late when they finally realize what they want," I added.

"So are you supporting this foolishness," Tavin said as he stood up from the table.

"I'm not, I'm just saying, that if Sammy likes a married guy that's cool for him, I can't change him." I said with guilt and in hopes he wouldn't have a negative perception of me.

"Well you can call it foolishness or whatever you like but right now I am seeing a married guy and there is no drama," Sammy added.

"It may be cool now but he will drop you because whether you like it or not, his wife comes first no matter what, you're just a piece of meat to him or a regular side fuck," said Tavin.

"NOW YOU ARE CROSSING THE LINE!"Sammy said in anger as he interrupted.

"Let me finish because I think you know that he will never love you, he just can't, its people like yourself who destroy the marriage homes, I hate when people cheat," Tavin completed.

"Okay okay this conversation just needs to stop please could we talk about something else" I quickly said before John could add in his two cents.

Sammy must have not gotten the hint, because he followed up his comment with a statement in Yoruba, so that Tavin couldn't understand. "So is Tavin trying to say he is holier than though? That he hasn't cheated before?"

I replied, "Well I really don't know about all that, I just think it's his opinion."

"Well all I am saying is tell your boyfriend I am watching him closely since he is very holy and has never cheated and he should stay away from criticizing me." Sammy said as he rolled his eyes, got up from the table in anger and walked towards the living room.

After a few hours I was glad it was just me and Tavin left in the room finally to talk. We talked a while about what had happened earlier and he told me he had gotten angry because he would hate for Sammy to influence me. I told him that I was old enough to know right from wrong. We fell asleep cuddling, but there was no sex. It wasn't even because of his HIV status; we were just learning how to enjoy one another's company.

That coming week Tavin moved into his new place.

I gave him the space I thought he needed to get settled in at his new home and I went on with my life preparing for the upcoming Christmas season and my birthday.

As my birthday approached, I was getting more and more excited because I was going to finally be legal. Thanks to Sammy, the arrangements had already been made for me to get into a club called the Bop House for free. At the last minute Tavin called and said that he wasn't feeling well enough to go out to the club, but that afterwards I could come by and spend the night with him. I was surprised, at my own reaction which was one of understanding. In the past I would have thrown a fit, regardless of someone's excuse if they did not make me the center of their world on a day like my birthday. But I knew he had been struggling as of late with his health and it made sense for him to lay low until he was feeling up to being around the crazy club crowd.

The club had two floors, one floor played nothing but hip hop music and the other floor was techno club beats. I could tell the minute we stepped in the club that the guys at this particular spot were more concerned about who was wearing what than about just letting loose and having a good time. By the look on Sammy's face after about an hour, I could tell he was ready to go. Around 1am, Sammy suggested we hit another club that was having a launch party that night.

The club was called Remake. When we entered Remake there were a good number of guys already on the dance floor. They also had go-go cages with guys in boy shorts and nothing else getting things jumping. One of the dancers had already caught my eye, so I headed over to see if I could support his cause by adding the ones in my pocket to the growing pile of money in his cage.

As I inched closer slowly making sure not to bump anyone's drink or step one any toes along the dance floor, he turned and to my surprise it was Aaron!

"TUNDE oh my god, I've been looking for you!" he shouted down to me over the din of the music.

But all said was, "Save it Aaron and get back to your job, these boys want to see a show."

"Fuck them I wanna talk with you," he said as he kneeled in the cage so I could hear him more clearly.

Aaron was nothing to me at this point after all he was one of those guys that you would hook up with your pet dog since they slept with anything that moved with a hole.

"No, I'm good Aaron," I said. "That chapter is closed."

As he was going to respond, a suited guy just as handsome walked up and said, "I don't pay you to chit chat with the customers, I pay you to move your ass."

I couldn't help but laugh, it served Aaron right, if I couldn't put him in his place there was always someone out there who could. I could tell that Aaron wanted to respond and say something to defend himself in front of me, but I didn't care. I just turned and walked off to go find Sammy. It felt good, getting a little of my power back.

By the time we left the second club, I was exhausted. I couldn't wait to curl up next to Tavin and go to sleep. I called him once I got outside the club, but the call went to voicemail. By this time, it was going on 3:30am, and I knew he was probably sleeping. I told Sammy to drop me off at Tavin's and I would catch up to him later on in the day.

"Are you sure," asked Sammy.

"Yeah, he told me to come over after we were done with our club hopping," I said.

"Ok, but if he didn't answer, you may as well just wait and catch up to him tomorrow," he said.

"No, I want to see him tonight. It's not like we are going to do anything, we haven't had sex the whole time."

"Yes, but still," added Sammy.

"Let me handle this," I said. "Just drop me off at my mans place."

"Ok miss thing," teased Sammy.

It's funny how the mind will play tricks on you when you are tired and focused on sleep. I didn't even see the other guy in the bed as I slid in next to Tavin.

20

Everyone cheats, I was convinced. The HIV status doesn't matter, where you come from doesn't matter and what you call yourself doesn't matter. Tavin had taught me that lesson. Here I was trusting in the fact that he had his head on his shoulders because he was struck with such a serious illness. But in the end, he was just playing a different sort of game, one that I hadn't yet received the rules for in order to play back.

I was determined to start playing a game of my own. It was time to get back to my computer and onward with my search.

Wassup my lil Nigerian,

I hope all is well with you man. Sorry I haven't connected with you in a while but I have been in and out of town and kind of busy. Right now I am in New York and headed for a three day trip. I still wanna hook up and meet you if that is cool. If so shoot me an

email and I promise to get back to you as soon as I can. Stay cute!

Calvin

This message was sent to my email address and not to one of my inboxes in a chat room. I got confused because I didn't remember this person at all but since he had known my email address I must have had a conversation with him at some point and time.

Since I couldn't remember him all I could do was reply saying "Ok cool Mister but I don't remember you."

I still had Tavin stuck in my memory. I wanted it out so I scheduled a few random visitors for some good all out sweaty sexcapades. I was sure a couple of dates were what I need to get the memory of Tavin out of my head. I don't even remember the name of the first guy. He came over within the hour of me contacting him. We both knew what he was there for and we wasted no time. I was already in my robe and nothing else when he arrived.

Once I led him into my bedroom, he reached into my condom jar which I kept on the floor next to my bed and took out a magnum. I proceeded to lie on my bed on my back watching him as he took off his pants and shirt.

He threw a lube pack on me and gave me a hand sign that signaled me to turn around and get in position. He didn't want foreplay and neither did I.

I got into position on my knees doggy style with my back arched, legs spread like I was doing a split in a dance show. He didn't even make any eye contact as I looked back while still in position. He stroked his dick, while he looked at my butt.

He slid in me so smoothly and I could feel my ass starting to get wet from excitement.

This guy was one of the guys they refer to as a homo thug. In the day he perpetrated like he was the next up and coming misogynist rapper and during the night, here he was balls deep in my ass. As he was pounding me from the back I had started to squeeze and stroke my manhood. I could feel myself about to come, but I wanted to hold off until I knew he was about to explode in me. I could feel his strokes getting shorter and more out of rhythm with each movement and I knew he would come any minute. I listened as his breath became more ragged and deep. I timed it perfectly, just as I felt my hands getting sticky and wet, I felt him shudder behind me and lean into me deeper.

As soon as he came, I told him goodnight and to lock the door behind him. He gave me an odd look, but did as he was told. I felt satisfied and fell asleep quickly, but right before I dozed off, Tavin's face formed right before me. I would need a couple more nights like this to make sure that didn't happen again.

It had been two days since my last dick down and I checked my email just to see if I had any messages and I did.

Wassup Cutie,

I know I am slow but I have been busy man. I am in transition to move back to Chicago and working from New York. My cell is 000 567 4411, leave a message or shoot me a text. I really don't check this email that often so try CalvinRowland @communicate.com I check this almost every day. Like I said before, I still want to meet your cute Nigerian ass! LOL... I love having friends of different nationalities! (wink)

Talk soon,
Calvin

For some reason I didn't respond maybe because I was tired of the games the games the online men played and I just wanted to be alone. But after awhile, I felt guilty not responding to his messages so I replied saying:

Hey sorry just been busy and haven't checked email for a while call me 010 888 9567.

I had to figure out who this Calvin was, so I went to his linked profile page from his email. His physical stats were age 32, height 6'1, weight 190lb, bald, mixed race and looking for friendship.

I finally got to find out who he was when he called me on my cell a few days later. I didn't recognize the number but as soon as I picked up and said, "Who is this?"

He responded, "Oh wow so you didn't save my number?"

Laughing I responded, "I'm sorry but who is this, I switched phones and I haven't saved all my contacts from the other phone."

"Hey, I'm at work right now, can you call me later?" I asked, stopping him from getting deeper into the conversation.

Later that night he called me and we talked about everything that there was to talk about. "I work as a flight attendant for a major airlines," he said.

As he was talking I was already imagining myself traveling the world, holding hands on a beach. I didn't even hear when he asked me a question until I heard, "Are you still there?"

"Yes I am sorry about that," I said.

"I was asking you to tell me more about yourself."

"I'm a regular college guy that works three jobs to survive and I'm here alone in the United States."

"You're here alone?"

"Where's your family?" he asked.

"My family is in Nigeria."

"So who did you stay with when you got here to the states? He asked.

"I was staying with my cousin when I first arrived in Chicago, but then I found a roommate."

"So tell me how many guys had you had sex with?"

"I think actually it's about twenty guys," I answered, but in reality I thought it may have been more than that.

"Twenty guys are u serious?" he asked.

"Wow I'm 32 and I have been with only three guys in my life time and your 21?"

I didn't know how to respond to his shock, so I sat there quietly on the phone waiting for him to continue.

"Well I'm not judging you I mean as long as you're using protection."

"Always," I said.

"So what school you go to?"

"I go to the Fashion and Arts School," I said.

"Really!?"

"Yeah I do," I said.

"I am glad we finally got a chance to talk today, I have to go now though, and I will hit you up when I get to New York."

"Ok, I don't want to hold you up," I said.

"So before I go, are you talking to someone else as well?" he asked.

"Yeah I am his name is Calvin and he is a flight attendant," I said smartly.

"You're crazy, but seriously I believe in talking to one someone and only that person," he emphasized.

"Oh ok that works for me, the less games the better," I sad.

"Well baby you should get some sleep for school tomorrow," he said.

"You're right about that it's about 2am here," I confirmed.

"G'night," he finished hanging up before I could return with one of my own.

I texted Sammy and John the next day telling them about Calvin and our conversation. But they both said the same thing, I should not fall so easily especially if I haven't met him but of course, I didn't listen to them.

During my first break between the morning classes, I headed over to the computer lab to see if I had any new emails from Calvin that day. I was not disappointed.

Hey,

I just got to my apartment in NYC and thought about you. I am excited about getting to know you and possibly starting something that will last a lifetime between us whether it is friendship or otherwise. You are definitely a cutie and I love your energy. I just hope that you are cool with what I do as far as career. Some guys can't handle the fact that my job requires me to be all over the world. I have spoken with a few colleagues who are in committed relationships and they informed me that their job is one of the spices that their partners enjoy doing with them. Some have said that they can't handle it... LOL.
I know this is all premature and everything. I just want you to be honest with me and allow me to be your friend first and foremost. This is the only guarantee that SOMETHING will last between us. Again, whether on a romantic level or platonic.

Think of me.... always.
Calvin

So I replied saying -

Hey Calvin,
First I want to say that I enjoy talking with you whether it's through text messages or on the phone. I agree that friendship is totally a base of something real and that will last long. Like I said communication and honesty as well as the right decisions will make things work. Lol your job does require you to be all over the world but its' what you love. For you to accept what I do as a person (performing etc) I think it gives me a clear signal that you are open so why shouldn't I let u do what you love. It may be tough but things could be worked out to our mutual satisfaction.

Tunde

I looked at his profile constantly from day to day. I would read his texts and IM's over and over again. I always thought that whenever I saw him in person for the first time, I would walk really slowly towards him to make the moment last.

He asked me to send him a current photo so that he could keep some on his phone. Took some the very day he asked for them and media mailed them to his phone. I thought I would have gotten a response back with compliments, but I didn't get anything back. I started to get nervous, thinking about whether or not I had gained too much weight or was my hair just right in the photo.

He finally texted back and said he had got them. I asked what he thought of the photos. I was floored by his response.

"I don't really like how you look now," he stated.

I was floored. Not that I thought everyone who came into contact with me should think I was a 10, but at least be tactful about the fact that you didn't. He told me he didn't like my long hair or my facial hair. He also went on to say that he preferred clean cut guys.

"When I saw your profile you looked different than what you do now," he continued. I was disappointed to say the least. Here he was having approached me out of the blue, and now all of a sudden I wasn't up to par with how he felt I should look. I knew better than to even attempt to change how I looked to appease him. I was happy with how I looked; I would just have to continue being patient.

21

I can honestly say that during my trial and fails at relationships, I never took my job or education very seriously. I couldn't I was too busy making sex my top priority. I couldn't help myself that if I had a guy telling me online that he was free at 1am and it was clashing with my sleep time for work or class the next morning, I would always tell the guy to come over because I didn't want to lose the opportunity of not meeting up with him.

I started to call off from work a lot and skip classes. Before, I had always been a 4.0 student. I didn't even tell my family back home that I was struggling to keep up with the other aspects of my life.

The warnings from my boss that I was neglecting the very simplest of tasks at work became more frequent. It wasn't much longer before I went in one day and within the hour they had fired me. That same week I applied for unemployment. All of my friends wondered the real reason I did not have a job and I just told them that I had been laid off due to low sales. Even when I had my interview for the unemployment benefits over the phone, he asked my reason for leaving and I lied again that I was laid off for not making enough sales. Little did I know that he would call back after their interview with me to say that my old job said it was because of my attendance that they had let me go.

I didn't have very many choices by way of income and I knew I had to make some money to be able to continue living in my apartment. So I turned to my best friend, the internet. I had always come across escort ads during my search to meet new guys. I decided to take a chance and place a couple of ads in the personal services section.

For the cleaning ad I wrote =

PROFFESIONAL YOUNG GAY COLLEGE BOY LOOKING FOR A REGULAR CLEANING JOB. AGE - 21 AND LOCATION - CHICAGO
Hello all,

I am looking to work for a very cool person that lives in the city. I am experienced at cleaning offices, hotels, homes, houses, apartments and condos. I will clean from the kitchen to the bathroom etc. I also can work and take care of pets. Hit me up for more info, thank you.

And my dancing ad read =

YOUNG BOY SEEKING TO PLEASE A GENEROUS MAN OF ANY AGE AND RACE
I am looking for a generous man tonight. I will meet with his complete satisfaction. Won't it be better to have someone give you a massage and a private show? Hit me up for more info, thank you.

I received the most interesting emails in answer to my ads. One man responded to my dancing ad and inquired how much I was charging. I responded and told him $150.00 and that payment needed to be made before performances. He replied in capital letters:

150???? AND NO SEX DUDE? WHAT THE FUCK OTHER GUYS ARE CHARGING $50 FOR SOME ASS FUCK OFF.

Then another response to my cleaning ad said:
Man all that sounds good but how much do you charge for cleaning? And do you clean in the nude? Or some kind of hot attire and is there some sex involved after you clean?

I replied that I charged $50.00 for every two hours of cleaning and to clean nude would be a separate fee of $80. I really just said that to scare him away from making me have to clean in the nude but instead of being dissuaded by my fees, he actually replied with his phone number and a time when I could come over!

Before I went over to his place for the cleaning job, I had already scheduled a dancing job for a guy that hadn't even asked how much I was charging and instead had just left a name and number in my email which in my mind kind of let me feel like he didn't care about the price..

So I went over to dance for him first. As soon as I walked in I headed straight to his bathroom and got to work. I dropped my clothes and put on my work attire which were very little boy shorts that had a special shaped cup for my package in front and at the back it left my ass hanging out.

I inserted my cd with my favorite playlist and I proceeded to drop it down low for him. The only close interaction I had with him was sitting on his lap and after about dancing to four songs; he paid me $250 plus a tip of $200 as well. He also asked me to come back and said that he enjoyed my dancing.

As soon as I left his place I headed over to the cleaning job I had booked. He was waiting for me downstairs at his apartment when I arrived. As soon as we got upstairs he directed me to where he wanted me to clean. I got to work right away, washing the few dishes that were in the sink and wiping down the countertops. I had come equipped with my own supplies even though he said he had a sufficient amount of cleaning supplies already. After the entire time I was cleaning, he stood in the doorway between the kitchen and the dining area watching me intently. I wasn't sure if he thought I was going to steal something or not. But I kept focused on my tasks at hand and didn't let it deter me. After about 15 minutes of me getting going in the kitchen, he said, "You look like you are sweating a little, why don't you take off your clothes so you can be comfortable?"

I put down the sponge I was using and proceeded to take off my polo shirt.

"Are you shy?" he asked.

"No," I said, looking directly at him.

"Then take it all off," he urged.

So I took off each layer of clothing I had on and stood naked in the middle of his kitchen.

"I didn't say for you to stop cleaning," he said calmly.

I turned around; picked up the sponge I had discarded and started wiping down the refrigerator before preparing to mop the floor. When I tried to bend over to grab my bucket, I could feel the bulge in his pants and he took his position directly behind me. From between my legs I could see his pants slowly sliding to the floor. I braced myself for what I knew would come next. In no time he was finished, I didn't even bother to tell him to put on a condom, and I was resigned about how my life was going to end up. After he was done, he handed me a $50 for the cleaning he said.

"As for the ass, you gave it willingly, so there is no pay for that."

I wasn't even upset about what he had said. I learned that for the next time, I needed to get paid first, for the cleaning and for the ass. There was definitely a lesson in every situation. The next time my ad was answered it was from a 52 yr old man in California that requested neither a cleaning nor a dance performance. He requested that I shit in a bag and send it to him. I must have read his email 10 times before I could muster the courage to write back to him. I thought it was some sort of odd joke that was being played on me. But no, he was serious; he sent me his phone number so that I could call him and get the specific instructions and details if I wanted the 'job'. I called him more out of shock than thinking I would actually go through with it. But when I called him I couldn't refuse his offer.

"Hi, can I speak to…uh?" I asked.

"Who is calling?" he asked in return.

"Uh… this is…you emailed me…uh my ad, you answered it," I finally said.

"Oh yes, yes, so you're interested?" he asked.

"Uh…I wasn't…didn't think," I said, sounding baffled the more I spoke.

"Look, if you do want the job, no questions," he instructed.

"Ok," I said.

"I will send you everything you need to get it collected," he added.

"And for each sample you provide, I will send you $700," he said.

"$700?," I asked and screamed.

"Yes," he confirmed.

I knew for sure I was being played. I thought back to my last cleaning job where I had been shorted for money, so I threw out there, "Well usually I get paid before I complete any work."

"That's not a problem," he said. "I will send you a wired deposit into your account."

"And that's all you want from me?" I asked still incredulous about the arrangement.

"Yes," he finished.

The next day $700 had been wired to my account which desperately needed the funds. Within the week I had received a parcel which contained a smaller package with an insulated bag in the smaller package. I couldn't believe it; I kept staring at the box and its contents on my living room table. I didn't know if I would be breaking any laws by doing what he requested, but since he had held up his end of the bargain and provided payment, I figured I had to comply with my end of the job.

I mailed off the package the next day and received an email of thanks from my California stranger.

By the following week another empty package had come in the mail once again and my account had been credited with $700. I was content with doing what he requested, I needed the money and who was I to judge regarding his particular fetish. It was none of my business, what was, was the money being put in my account.

22

I was an addict. I was so deep into my addiction that I couldn't quite figure out how to get out of the life I had created for myself. The money was too good to turn down and since I still wasn't ready to give up the internet just yet, there was no way I was going to be able to hold down a regular job. I would simply find myself in the same situation I was in before to get fired. I was not calling it what it was, I was cruising the internet and battling with my personal demons.

The lines were so blurred for me I couldn't figure out if I even believed I was still looking for love in my searches or whether it was just sex masked as something else.

There was no shortage of men to feed my needs. I could log on at any time of the day or night and there would be someone there willing to exchange information in hopes of eventually hooking up. That Monday for me was just such as day. I was logging on to find out who the next best thing would be for the day. The first email I opened was actually from someone I had met the prior week. I thought he was calling to hook up again, I knew I was that good. But he wasn't contacting me about a hook-up; he was telling me that I had given him an STD. I emailed him back immediately and told him that was not a very funny joke. And that if he was serious he needed to check into the other guys he had messed with and not me. I knew I didn't have anything.

He replied back and requested my contact information so he could provide it to his doctor. He also recommended I contact any other guy I may have had sex with to let them know. I wasn't going to give him any of my information; I didn't want him to post anything about me on the website saying I had a disease.

He emailed me again when I didn't reply to his last message. He said he remembered that after I had left his place and he had cleaned up after me that my semen had left an odd colored stain on his sheets. I didn't want to read anymore of his lies so I signed off the computer and refused to give any of what he had said a second thought.

The next day I called Sammy to discuss the emails I had received. I was partially scared to find out if in fact anything was wrong with me. I simply wanted the emails to disappear and to forget he had even contacted me.

"Don't be stupid Tunde," Sammy said.

"Go get checked out," he added.

"Yes, but I know I don't have anything," I said feebly.

"Oh really, when did you get your degree in medicine?" asked Sammy.

"You know what I mean," I continued. "I would know if I had something."

The only way I could get Sammy off the phone that day was to tell him I would make sure and get an appointment to see the doctor. Even though I had no intention of doing anything of the sort, I knew I was fine. It's funny how the mind will start to convince you of something you haven't done. I started replaying all the times I had been having sex and how every time I had used a condom.

Now I had another title I could attribute to my behavior, at least in private, denial.

23

July 27th 2009 was my point of no return. I had logged on to Black Gay Convo and the site administrator had posted a video in the open forum section. In the video they were giving national statistics on where gay men fell for contraction of HIV/AIDs. In Chicago alone it said that 1 in 5 gay men in Chicago had HIV. Seeing that simple video built a fear in me so strongly that I could do nothing but replay the video several times.

For me it wasn't just that I had unprotected sex or that I had sex with many guys but that I was statistically amongst the gay men that didn't know their status at all.

I made an appointment the next day at the Neighborhood Med Center to get tested. I even recruited Sammy to come along with me for moral support.

When we arrived there were already a few people waiting ahead of me. I was hoping they weren't going to ask me any questions that I would have to answer out loud in front of everyone in the waiting room. I signed my name on the list located at the reception desk and waited for my name to be called.

"Tandie." announced the nurse that emerged from the exam room door.

I raised my hand and said, "Tunde," emphasizing the *u* pronunciation to her.

Sammy laughed from behind me when she mispronounced my name. Leave it to him to find humor in my nerve-racking ordeal.

"Here goes nothing," I said to him, shrugging my shoulders.

When the nurse had placed me in a room, she started asking me the usual questions, when did I last have sex, how many partners did I have in the past few months, did I always use protection and what exactly brought me to the office today. I answered each question honestly; I was tired to lying about all that I had done. It was time to take care of myself.

"I would like to get tested," I said resigned.

"Ok, we have a quicker way to test now," she said. "It's a simple process and you can just relax," she continued.

In no time, my blood was drawn and I was told to go and have a seat in the waiting room. They said they would have my results in approximately 20 minutes. They were the longest twenty minutes of my life. Even Sammy in his usual jovial state seemed strained as we sat their quietly in the waiting room. When the nurse finally called my name again to let me know the results, it seemed like hours had gone by in that room. She took me to the back in the same room where I was tested and told me that my results were negative. I had never been so relieved in all of my life. I hadn't realized exactly how much I wanted to live until I had to wait for those twenty minutes to go by to get the results.

When I came outside and told Sammy, he gave me a big hug and told me he was proud of me for taking the first step in regaining control of my life.

Since I had already taken the major step, I decide to go a step further and get an entire STD screening completed.

I headed over to the regular clinic which was located in the same medical complex to get my STD screening done. I was feeling a little more confident so I told Sammy he didn't have to stay with me for the rest of the testing.

This waiting room was even more packed than the first. Everyone had that look on their face that questioned, 'And what exactly are you here for?' I simply wanted to get it all over with and get assurance that everything was ok.

Once they had done the needed blood draws, I was told that it would take approximately a week to get the results back from my screening. I was ok with that; I had had enough excitement for one day.

When the clinic called me to let me know the results of from my battery of tests, I thought they were going to be able to tell me over the phone. But I was told that I had to come down to get my results in person. I was sure it was just a formality so I headed down there the next morning. Sure enough, my tests came back positive for Syphilis and Chlamydia.

I was told that I would be prescribed antibiotics and have to return for follow up treatment. I was embarrassed and felt dirty, but I was ready to deal with it head on. It was a better diagnosis than I had originally feared and I would grow up and deal with it as I needed.

I remembered as I was waiting to get my results, there were two of the regulars from the club scene who I knew by name. But when we were in that waiting room all together, none of us spoke to one another.

It had been going on a month and I hadn't had sex. I never knew I could hold out that long without having sex, but I did and I was proud of myself. But there was that side of me, which was willing to take a chance again. After all, I had received notice of what was ailing me and I could do nothing but start fresh, make sure and use condoms and I would be back on top again.

24

I missed it; I missed the excitement of getting an inquiry or an email, talking to someone new and meeting up for the first time.

My journey back to the sites this time around would be a bit more interesting than the previous, well so I always said to myself. I was giving my body to anybody that met my definition of sexy.

When Sammy or John would question why I kept returning to the sites I would say, "If someone like me is on the site, it means I might have a chance at finding love."

They both said the same thing, that they weren't trying to change me but they were tired of me complaining about the same treatment when it was me placing myself in those situations.

What neither of them understood was that there were times when finding someone online to hold me for at least the night was more companionship than I thought I could ever hope to get. It was vital to my existence and I was willing to make sacrifices in order to get that, even if just for a night.

Roi was just such a sacrifice. I could see that he had reviewed my profile several times online before contacting me. So at least this time, unlike with Calvin, I was sure he knew what I looked like and that my looks were acceptable to him.

We didn't waste a lot of time with back and forth emails or lengthy phone calls. We knew we were both interested in one another early on and we threw caution to the wind and met up in person by the third day of conversing. He was handsome in a conventional and simple way. There were no bulging muscles and he didn't necessarily exude sexuality when you saw him in person, but there seemed to be a kindness about him which was what made him attractive.

By the following Friday of the second week of us talking, I found myself packing clothes to stay over his house for the weekend. I let Sammy and John know where I would be for that weekend, just in case. Although I didn't sense that I had anything to worry about. After I had packed, I headed downstairs to wait, but I didn't have to wait for very long, because there he was waiting in his silver Range Rover at the curb in front of my building.

As I walked towards him, he leaned over towards the passenger door to open in from the inside for me.

"Hi," I said as I got in and sat in the passenger's side seat.

"Hey there handsome," he replied, waiting for me to get my seatbelt on before he pulled off.

"So where exactly is it that you are kidnapping me to?" I teased. I had texted Sammy that I would get him all the vital information before I left the city.

"It's a surprise," he stated.

"So are you living with your family?" he asked, changing the subject.

"No," I answered. "They are all still back in Nigeria, I'm the only one here."

"So you came from Nigeria to America to stay with who?" he asked again, thinking he hadn't asked the question clearly enough.

"To stay with my crazy cousin, until I got on my feet," I answered more specifically.

"And why is he or she crazy?" he asked smiling.

"It's a she, and I really don't want talk about it," I finished.

"Ok, I didn't mean to pry," he apologized.

"No worries," I said. "I would rather talk about a pleasant topic, that's all."

"So you said love was one of the things you were looking for, have you found it yet?"

"No I haven't found it with any of the people I have met over the years, and at this point I just don't care anymore," I said, sounding a little more than resigned.

"Well you might be looking at love right now," he replied confidently. Something in me wanted to laugh hysterically in his face at that, but I refrained.

"That's what they all say," I said instead.

"Please don't compare me to those other guys you have met," Roi stated.

"I was just saying that's what I have been through," I replied.

"So what kinds of guys do you like any way?" he asked.

"I don't think I really have a type of guy, I'm open I guess," I said, sounding a little disappointed in my own lack of specifics. Maybe that was why I was getting every and anything other than what I needed, I didn't have any specifics to judge people under.

"Of course you have a type," he said.

"Well, then maybe I don't know what it is then," I said. "So if I was 300 pounds with a jhery curl and wore tight clothes and was feminine would you still follow me home?"

"NO I would not!" I exclaimed giggling.

"Oh so you do have a type then," he finished, emphasizing his point.

"I guess I like more masculine guys that know what they want out of life," I said.

"Very interesting."

"Yes it is, so do you consider yourself masculine?" I asked.

"So far what do you think? You tell me."

"I am just me."

"I am who I am just like you are down low." I said really getting the conversation jumping.

I could tell by the way he gripped the steering wheel he was annoyed by my forward assessment and assumption of him.

"What do you mean down low?" he asked.

"C'mon, I know you are probably still running game on women...tell me you aren't?" I asked and answered

"I wouldn't say that I was *down low*," he said, emphasizing the last part.

"I'm discreet," he added. "Discreet means you are ok with people knowing your gay sometimes, you might attend gay public events. Down low to me is you are totally locked in the closet from anyone knowing who you really are and are actively in relationships with women."

"That's your definition and if you are going to be with me you have to be masculine for me to be with you," I said.

"Are you gay or bisexual?" I asked not caring about whether I was pushing the envelope of topics with him.

"I would say that I am straight because I have never had sex with a guy and I am actually trying to go out with this lady at my job."

"Then that would mean that you're bisexual because clearly you are not new to Black Gay Convo."

"I am straight no matter what you think and I am taking you home to just spend time with you and talk not to have sex," he said.

I could tell this one was going to be one to remember. He was in denial about his sexuality, but still wanting to have his cake and eat it to, guys like this always confused me. I was ready to be at our destination, I was really curious as to how the night was going to unfold. It talk only was really what was on his mind.

"It sounds like you travel a lot from what you have on your description, have you ever been to Nigeria?" I asked changing the subject again.

"Yes I have for about two months."

"Did you enjoy it?"

"Yes I did and the people were very respectful and nice to me when I was there," he added.

"Have you been back since you came to the US?" he asked.

"No, I'm a student and that's a pretty big expense, at this point I am not sure when I will go back," I answered. Talking about Nigeria always brought me back to thinking about my mom. Sooner or later I would have to tell her everything about my life. Even though my family didn't love close by, I still felt sad for having to live deceptively.

"Your parents won't pay for you to come back?" he asked.

"Well my mother said she would buy the ticket for me, but that would require me to get my passport in order as well and I just haven't had the time to do it yet."

"You should get on it; don't you miss your country?"

"I do, but school has been crazy and I still need to find another job."

"Don't worry, when you get to finally know the real me and you are mine, you won't have to work," he said.

I had heard this before, it didn't really impress me. What would impress me was if he was to admit to being Gay. But I didn't say anything to his premature proposal. I just nodded and smiled.

"Oh is that coming from the straight guy that denied being bisexual earlier?" I said after a while of silence. I couldn't resist continuing to push his buttons.

"You have a very sharp mouth," he said laughing.

"Yes I do since I am my own being and I pay my own bills," I said.

"So where are you from?" I asked.

"I'm also from Africa," he answered.

I couldn't tell if he was playing around with me or not. He didn't have any distinguishable emotion on his face. He didn't have any kind of accent not even a British one which many Africans had if they had spent any time there before coming to the US.

"What part of Africa?" I quizzed still doubting his authenticity.

"I'm not from Nigeria if that's what where you were thinking,"

"Well then, what part?"

"I'm from Liberia."

"Oh that's nice but I still don't think you're telling me the truth." I said flatly.

I hadn't been paying very much attention as he was driving where exactly we were headed to, but as soon as I recognized that he gotten into the Evanston area of Chicago, I started to look out for the cross street names so I could text Sammy my exact location. But as he drove from street to street continuously it felt like he was either lost or intentionally driving like that so I wouldn't be able to recall the way to his house.

When he finally turned down his street he parked a few houses down. We got out and he grabbed my back from the backseat of his car. He started walking towards a blue house with white trim which was two houses down from where we parked. I was wondering why he hadn't just parked in the driveway itself, it would have made more sense. As we entered his home, he removed his shoes and I could hear him say over his shoulder, "Tunde, please take your shoes off here at the door."

"You have a beautiful place," I said. "But it looks empty."

"Yes I just moved in like I told you."

"Cool."

"What do you want to drink?"

"Anything you have."

"Well, make yourself at home; you're welcome to use the computer if you want. I know you probably want to check your messages on BGC," he said smiling.

"No I don't actually," I said laughing. "I'm not that addicted to it, am I?" I asked.

He shrugged and smiled shaking his head at me.

"I have cranberry juice and I have iced tea," he yelled from the kitchen. I walked around the living room and took at look at some of the books he had sitting on his coffee table. Most were about financial topics and investing.

"Cranberry juice is fine with me," I answered.

"I don't have TV yet," he said walking back into the living room with the glass of juice in his hand. "I hope that's going to be ok with you."

"I can do without a TV," I said. "It's the internet that I can't do without."

"So how often are you in the chat room?" I asked.

"I go on almost every day, but I don't talk to just everyone on there," he said. "I have one regular guy that I check in with, and then every now and again I will answer an ad."

"Oh, is it a potential love interest that you talk to all the time?" I asked feeling a little pang of jealousy.

"No, it's he's just my friend. I was touched when he shared his story with me about having been raped and contracting HIV from his rapist."

"That's really sad," I said thinking back to my London experience. "People are crazy."

"Yes it was actually a guy he met online. He had travelled to meet the guy in another state when he was only sixteen."

I wasn't yet ready to tell anyone about what I had went through in London. I didn't feel like being judged or told that I was stupid for going on and meeting someone in a country I knew nothing about. It was something I told myself regularly but still didn't heed the warning.

Roi and I sat there and talked from one topic to the next. He was very attentive but I knew he was someone that I could never be in a relationship with in the long run. He wasn't really my type, but I would have sex with him. I was already there and despite his statements about not bringing me to his home for sex, I knew what he would ultimately want from me.

Around 11pm, Roi said we could go into his bedroom and continue talking. He also said that if I wanted to sleep in the nude I could and that he wouldn't touch me or make any advances. I didn't believe him, I knew he was just too shy to just come out and say what it was he wanted. But I was up for the game so I went ahead and took off all of my clothes and got into the bed. He wore his boxer briefs to bed. When I got in I turned so that I was facing him.

He was lying on his back with one arm behind his head. I gently shifted in the bed, making sure that my knee brushed against his thigh. I could feel him tense up in anticipation for what was to come next. But I didn't let him off the hook that easily.

"So tell me about Liberia," I said. Throwing him totally off.

"What do you want to know about it?" he asked.

"What was it like growing up there?" I asked.

"Well, I didn't really grow up there, I grew up in the US," he said.

I was good, I knew he wasn't African; it didn't really count if you were born and raised here. Even though I was born here I was raised in Africa, I could probably tell him more about Liberia than he could tell me.

I didn't bother rubbing it in; it was enough knowing that I was right.

I shifted slightly again, making sure the contact between my knee and his thigh remained intact. I thought for sure he would be more of a challenge. But the minute the sheet tented around his erection, I knew I had him.

I took advantage of his vulnerable state and I moved closer to him and placed my hand on his stomach just above his erection in a semi hug. I could feel his whole body tense up even further. His breathing was now low and measured. He was definitely trying to remain in control, but I knew it wouldn't last for very long.

He must have been having a conversation about restraint in his own head, because he had a focused expression on his face and he was staring straight up at the ceiling.

I moved my arm to grab his waist tight and made sure to accidently brush against his erection with my forearm.

That was the straw that broke the camel's back because he became alert from his stupor and rolled over to face me. He didn't even try to hide his urgency; he grabbed me closer and aggressively grabbed my ass with his free hand.

He started licking my neck and shoulder as he grabbed me tighter. I was never big on licking but I allowed him to as I moaned approval to encourage him. In the meantime I wanted to see what Roi had to offer, so I slid my hand down and into his briefs. I was disappointed; he was quite small in comparison to the other guys I had been with in the past. But at least it had girth. Hopefully he knew how to work the little that he had and would not let me down.

I didn't see any nightstand next to his bed, the usual hiding spot for all the goodies, so I had to ask.

"Where do you keep your condoms and lube?" I said.

"What?" he asked in return.

"Condoms, lube?" I asked again. "Never mind, I have some," I said before he could respond again. I made sure and carried a little sex kit with me now after my scare with the STD. I didn't want to have to see the inside or a clinic again unless it was yearly regular health check-up.

I went back out to the living room and grabbed my shoulder bag to grab my little kit from inside. In it I had condoms, sample sized packets of lube and wipes. When I came back to the bedroom, he was stroking his dick, waiting for me.

I hopped on the bed and he was one me before I could even get settled. He rolled me over and got on top of me spreading my legs simultaneously. I had just enough time to hand him the condom and put on some lube. With no foreplay he entered me in one motion. He had his hand on the back of my head which forced me to arch my back more so that my ass was almost up in the air.

He was really going at me; his hands were now on my hips holding me tightly in one place. Even though he was small, I could feel all of him swell in me. He came and let out a big grunt as his entire body relaxed against me. I had already come, but I was doing my duty and letting him finish properly. My back was covered in his sweat from his workout. When he was finished, I pushed away so he could slide out and I headed for the shower. I wasn't even remotely interested in having any after sex chat or recap of what had just happened.

Once I had finished showering, I walked out of the bathroom still drying myself off. Roi was still laying there on the bed in the same position I had left him in stroking his dick again. I gave him a look of disgust as I finished drying off and putting on my clothes.

"Why are you looking at me like that?" he asked.

"Like I think you're crazy?" I asked.

"Well if that's what you want to call it then yes," he said.

"Because you just came aren't you going to clean up and go to sleep?" I asked.

"I'm not done yet, I come more than once," he boasted proudly.

"Oh really well in this case you will not come more than once in me because I'm tired and about to go sleep," I said.

I got into the bed but sat up this time so he wouldn't think I was playing around and flirting like I had the first time around.

"C'mon just let me come for the second time," he said.

"Actually you weren't supposed to come the first time," I said. "Aren't you the one that just wanted to talk the whole weekend?" I reminded him.

"Don't be a smart ass," he replied.

"I'm not; I was just reminding you of your original goal for this weekend."

"Just little bit more Tunde," he begged.

"No Roi," I answered.

My mood was beginning to sour. I hated when a man begged for it. To me it showed that he was desperate and not confident in simply taking it. I don't know if I would have ever allowed Roi to just take it, but there were definitely guys who I didn't mind being forceful with me. He was not one of them. By the third or fourth no, I was just that I was not feeling him. His mood also changed. He rolled over pouting, but still continued to stroke his dick. I could hear him come after a few minutes and wondered why he hadn't gotten up to still clean himself.

After a few minutes it didn't matter much to me what he was doing because before I knew it I was in a deep sleep. I awoke the next morning to the sun streaming in through the window. He wasn't next to me, I could hear the shower going and he was humming to himself. I was ready to go home. Since I had already taken a shower the night before I started getting dressed. I could still hear him in the shower humming away by the time I was fully dressed.

I decide to take a mini tour of the house since I hadn't had one the night before. After that I would head into the kitchen to see if there was anything instant that I could eat. Walking down the hall, there were all sorts of awards that hung on the both sides of the wall. Some were honors he had received and others were degrees from various stages in his education. As I was inspecting the awards I heard the bathroom door open.

"Tunde?" I heard him call out.

"Yeah, I'm out here," I answered.

"Ok, just give me a second, I'm almost done," he said.

I finished reading the plaques and then headed to the kitchen to wait for him.

"You must be hungry," he said as he entered the kitchen.

"Not really," I said. Thinking maybe he would just take me home.

"What do you usually eat at home in the mornings?" he asked.

"Actually I don't eat in the mornings and if I do maybe some cereal or toast," I answered.

"Well I wanted to make you a nice traditional African breakfast," he said.

"Or have you have forgotten because you have been Americanized?" he added.

"I haven't forgotten or been Americanized," I said. "But it's just breakfast food and my mom always cooked pancakes and other things even when we were in Africa."

"And the other days what did you eat?" he asked, not letting the subject go.

"Mostly I would eat yam and eggs or agege bread with sardine or eggs," I said.

"Well I am cooking some potatoes and meat stew," he responded.

"Ok sounds good," I said giving in.

"What are you doing today?" I asked.

"I'm going to spend it with you," he said.

"Aww that's sweet but I really need to do a job search today and finish some of my school assignments that I haven't completed yet," I said.

"Is that your way of running from me because I'm boring you?" he asked.

"No it's not but I need a job badly, my phone bill is coming up soon and my rent is overdue."

We talked about light topics as he was making breakfast. I asked about more of his life in Liberia which he was really vague about and said he didn't remember much. It seemed strange because every African I meet always knows about what's going on in their country whether they've been back or not. He wanted to talk more about his many investments and what his goals were for settling down in Chicago.

Once he had finished cooking, we ate and he asked me about school and how much longer I had to go. I had to admit the breakfast was pretty good and it did hit the spot even thought I didn't really want to admit that to him. The seasonings he had used reminded me of ones that my mom used in Nigeria. After breakfast I offered to help him wash the dishes and get the kitchen straightened. But he said he could take care of it later, that he would take me home as I had requested. I was grateful that I would soon be back at my place and I could be done with this weekend away trip.

The ride home was fairly quiet. Asides from him asking if I needed anything, I sat there quietly and watched the city go by as we headed to my apartment. Even when we got to the front of my building he asked if he was going to be able to see me again and I responded maybe. I knew that he knew we would never see each other again. Or maybe he did hold out some hope, but I didn't care either way. I gave him a light hug goodbye and got out of the car.

I didn't even look back or wave as he was driving off. When I was done, I was done. I went upstairs and crashed on my bed for next four hours.

When I finally woke up, I saw that I had four missed calls and one text message. Two of the calls and the text message were from Roi. Sammy has also called and the last number was a blocked caller ID. I deleted everything and called Sammy back to update him about the latest events of my life.

It was Sammy that suggested that I search for him on the internet. He said it sounded odd that he was so vague about Africa even though he had mentioned being from Liberia. I told him it didn't matter either way to me; I wasn't planning on seeing him anymore.

"Then just do it for the hell of it," Sammy said. "I searched for this guy one time and it turned out he was working for IRS!" Leave it to Sammy to be nosing around about where someone worked. I figured there was no harm in being nosey myself. Except I couldn't remember what his last name was, so I logged on to see if I had saved his email msgs so I could looked it up. I had deleted them but they were still in my trash folder.

I was surprised; he was telling the truth about being from Africa. And the placards that were on his wall at his home were an understatement compared to all the other accomplishments he had attained.

The first article caught my attention, and it talked about his affiliation with the military in Liberia. The article talked about how he was a man that had even saved the lives of others during various combat situations. He had even founded a humanitarian organization after leaving the military. The really shocking part was that he had twelve kids with his wives and three adopted children! I wondered if any of them knew about his secret life here in the US. Of course, I was no better to judge, no one in Nigeria knew what I was doing here either, but at least I didn't have any children and definitely no wives.

While I was searching for the information about Roi, I wondered how many other high profile men where on these sites. If you were like me and didn't necessarily keep up with who all the upper crust people were, it was possible to meet up with someone like Roi and not know any differently.

I was never one to necessarily chase the status or the money of someone I dated. It was always fun to get spoiled by someone but I felt like I had the capability if I put my mind to it to spoil them in the same manner. I wasn't looking to be a kept man even though I liked getting the promises that I wouldn't have to work or that I could live a life of leisure if I allowed the 'right' man to have me.

25

After dealing with Roi, and having a few other no frills date nights that ended in me showering and taking leave. I started thinking maybe it was ok to hold out for a guy that had the means to take care of me. My friend Kolawole had lucked out and had a guy who was willing to pay for tickets for his friends to fly out to visit him. I could probably get the same thing if I tried hard enough and elevated my expectations. If they were going to be offering, there was nothing wrong with me taking.

My latest conquest wasn't a high profile guy. But he was definitely my most erotic one. Eddy was 32, 5'11", 212lbs, muscular, looking for friendship and was about to meet me. I had seen his pic and was immediately attracted. He never did email me back after my initial inquiry email to him. Not that I was expecting him to, I had just came right out in the email and told him I liked his photos and that I wanted to see if we had anything in common. I also had sent my phone number in that first email. I was beyond the back and forth long drawn out roundabout that would normally happen. It was all so silly when we got right down to it.

Eddy called me for the first time at 4:15 am told me his wife had headed to work and that she was a nurse so I could come over. And that was it, there was no preamble chit chat, now how are you or anything to the conversation.

I thought it was too late for me to try and get over there, but before I could even tell him it was too late he had hung up. He called me the next day and said I had wasted time in thinking about it instead of simply responding with a yes. Instead he had gotten someone else who was quicker on the draw to coming over.

The first time we did finally meet it was a virtual meeting. His wife was out of the house and he wanted to do a webcam virtual hook-up and mutual masturbation while we watched one another. I thought the concept was hot and complied with his request. It was erotic to watch him on the screen with me on the other end grabbing my member and caressing it to match the strokes he was issuing to his. When he started to moan on the other end it was too much for me to hold back. I came so hard that my eyes got teary as I was ejaculating.

I never actually got a chance to meet Eddy in person but we talked a lot online virtually when his girlfriend wasn't at home. He lived in Hyde Park and I never wanted to head that far away from my home, on the train, in the middle of the night when his girl was at work just to get some dick. Not when I could call for a closer dick down right around the corner. Instead I reveled in the live porn we would perform for each other, it was the safest sex I ever had.

Then one day he left me a message telling me he was deleting his profile because he had found the right bottom that could be a regular for him.

I was disappointed about our short-lived webcam adventures more so that I had been about all my other in person outings with guys.

Like my friend Sammy would always say, "Once you taste good dick you can't help but to keep ordering."

26

My friends were starting to ask me if I had found someone special yet or if I at least had any strong possibilities. I would always say no, not yet. Their response always made me feel embarrassed and saddened about the condition of my life. They would say, "Out of all the boys you have on speed dial, there is no one that seems like a potential partner, what are you doing Tunde?"

And they were right but I called it living my life so I wouldn't feel like I was passing myself around like a remote. I noticed that my encounters were getting more desperate. Even if the guy wasn't what I was necessarily looking for, I would entertain the sex. There were clearly some guys who I shouldn't have even wasted the gigabytes on when emailing, but I did out of that small chance, that maybe, maybe this one is the one for me, despite appearance and glaring warnings. It was under this desperation that I ended up in the hospital being asked by a patient if I would give him a hand job.

I had followed my daily routine and got online. Getting online now was like making breakfast for me. I wasn't eating or taking care of myself and I wasn't doing the usual things that people would do because I was so concerned with having missed a message or not having answered a message in time before the guy moved on to another ad.

He seemed to be in a rush because when I emailed him I said

—

Me: Hi how are you today

Him: What's your name and number because I would love to hook up for a hand job if you are game

Me: I'm always game, but is that the only thing we are going to do?

Him: No, after you give me a hand job, I am going to bend you over and fuck that wet ass of yours, then I am going to come in your mouth before I bend you back over and fuck you again.

When I saw all he had wrote of course I didn't bother to think it through. I just assumed this person was like me, someone who enjoyed sex and who needed it ASAP like a calm down pill.

I gave him my phone number and within seconds he called and gave me his address and told me to come over. I didn't skip a beat or waste any time heading over to the address he had provided. By this time, the concept of texting Sammy to let him know where I was in case something happened had long been abandoned. I am sure Sammy was probably tired of my almost nightly texts describing someone knew who I was going off with to who knows where.

There was something more important I was supposed to have been doing at that time which was meeting my classmates for a group study session. But I disregarded that and headed to my latest rendezvous. As I got closer to my destination, I started looking ahead to see if I could determine which specific building the address lead to. But when I got in front of the building it wasn't an apartment building or a house. It was the downtown public hospital. I texted him to make sure I had the right address and that I was in the right place. He texted me back right away and said yes and gave me a specific room number. I had heard of stranger things happening, but I thought maybe it was a nurse or a doctor who was trying to get one in before they had to go on shift or something. So I went to the bank of elevators to head up to the 10th floor where room 1010 was located. When I stepped off the elevator there were double doors which said they lead to 'Patient Rooms 1000 – 1030.

At this point you would think I would have turned back around but in all honesty, I still kept thinking about the 13inch dick status he had on his profile. I headed through those double doors and down the hall with the room numbers until I found 1010. When I stopped in front of the door I had thoughts of Tavin thinking maybe it was him trying to get in contact with me again after his cheating episode. I pushed open the door and hear my name being called.

"Tunde?!"

"Yes?"

"Pull the curtain closed behind you and come sit here," he said tapping the bed next to him.

It wasn't Tavin, it was the guy in the photo on the profile, but he wasn't staff at the hospital, he was a patient.

I was trying to quickly take in the scene that was in front of me and still put two and two together. He was lying in bed with a drip attached to the back of his hand and he had one of his legs in a cast which was hooked to a strap support dropped from the ceiling of the room.

I couldn't believe this was happening.

"Come sit down," he said again patting the empty spot on the bed next to him.

"You... can't... be... serious... right?" I said slowly.

"Why not?" he asked. "There's nothing wrong with my penis, it's my leg that's broken."

I didn't even turn back around as he called my name when I opened the door to leave. I felt like running away and never coming back not even to my apartment.

I realized that night that sometimes rock bottom comes up to meet you half way.

27

Even after my failed hospital rendezvous, I kept going back for more. I had fooled myself into thinking that if I changed the parameters of my search I would have better luck. There are those of us that have to learn life's lessons the hard way. Even when that small voice is telling you to make a different choice and you hush it because you feel you know best than that inner voice. You still go forward into the situation that could possibly define your point of no return. I had already experienced a scare, but it didn't stop me, I took it as a short pausing point on my path for total destruction.

My last sexual encounter was one that I remember most vividly. I had been pursuing this guy online for months. We would make plans to get together and then something would happen in his or my schedule and we would make an attempt to reschedule and it would never happen.

I finally convinced him to come over one night when it was raining. It took him about 2hrs to get to my place when he had originally told me he could be there in thirty minutes. He requested I only wear a white tank, grey boxers and socks when he came. I was always an obedient and willing sexual partner so I did as I was told. I didn't make any requests of him except for him to simply come over. I kept a look out from my window to make sure I would see him approaching so that I could go downstairs and let him in. Since it was raining, he told me he would be wearing a grey trench coat and he gave me a general description of himself to jog my memory about how he looked.

I saw when he hit the corner of my block and started heading in the direction of my building. There weren't that many people out on my street and he was the only one wearing a trench coat. I headed downstairs to let him in. By the time I made it downstairs he was just turning the corner to come into the outer lobby of my building. I buzzed the entry bell and he pushed the door gently to come into where I was standing waiting for him. He looked tired but basically the same way in which he had described and seeing him brought back memories of when I had first seen his photo online except now he looked a bit thinner in person even though I couldn't see fully his body due to the coat.

We exchanged greetings and I lead him over to the elevator which would lead to my floor and on to my apartment. When we got into the elevator I noticed there was a slight odor about him. But I attributed it to him having to walk and probably sweating from the Chicago humidity when it rained. It was noticeable but not repulsive.

As we excited the elevator I allowed him to get off of the elevator first so that I could hold the door to the elevator open for him and it not close on his as he was getting out as it was known to do if you were taking your time getting on or off.

When he passed me I saw that there was a big rip on the back of his trench coat and it looked overall somewhat dingy in the light.

When we got into my apartment, I told him to make himself at home and asked if he wanted anything to drink. But he said that he had just eaten and didn't want anything.

I was offering out of expected obligation because my fridge was empty except for the box of baking soda at the back of the fridge. If he had accepted my offer I would have had to go to the corner store to get him something. He took a seat on my couch and I sat next to him so we could play a little catch up before we headed into my bedroom. I offered to take his coat but he said he was cold and wanted to keep it on until we were ready to go to bed. It didn't seem like he was in any rush to head to the bedroom so I offered to put a movie in the DVD player.

He was ok with that so I put in a scary movie thinking that would expedite cuddling on the couch. My phone kept going on notifying me that I had new messages in my email inbox. I eventually turned it off so it wouldn't appear to him like I was hooking up with every that crossed my path. I had dimmed the light in my living room to create somewhat of a mood which is when he finally agreed to take off his coat. I took his coat and hung in up in my hallway coat closet and as I would hanging it up the movement of the material definitely carried some kind of odor. Before the scent hadn't been so offensive when he was still wearing it, but now with the garment standing alone there was a strong odor which I couldn't quite place but that I had definitely come into contact with before.

He kept asking to go to the bathroom; I wasn't sure if it was just nerves or if he simply had a weak bladder. I could also tell that he sounded a little nasally as though he had just gotten or was getting over having a cold.

When he returned from the bathroom for the last time, this time he made sure and sat closer to me on the couch. I leaned into him to let him know it was ok to get closer and he placed his arm on my shoulder. That scent was still there underlying but I thought it was definitely attributed to the coat and not his person.

I put my head on his shoulder and he tilted my head up and back and gave me a light kiss. I had started wondering if things would ever get going with us, so I was happy to see he was at least warming up to the encounter. After the first kiss we went back to watching the movie and I continued lying against him. When the movie was over I asked him if he wanted me to put in another one.

"No," he said.

"Do you want to go into the bedroom so we can get comfortable?" I asked.

"Sure, that would be good," he said. He said he had to go to the bathroom again and would meet me in the bedroom. While he was in the bathroom I headed to my bedroom to make sure that I had cleared everything off my bed. Since I knew where things were going to be headed, I went ahead and took off my clothes and got into bed and waited for him to join me.

When he finally came out of the bathroom and into the bedroom, he smiled when he saw me in the bed.

"Get comfortable," I said.

"Do you mind if I turn out the lights?" he asked.

"Go ahead," I said. "I can still work it in the dark."

He didn't answer, but complied and started taking off his clothes. Even in the dark I could still tell from the street light streaming through my window that he was taking off more than just the clothes I could visible see that he had on. He hadn't even gotten into taking off his pants and I could tell that he had taken off approximate three layers of shirts that were almost twice his size.

I had dated guys who refer to themselves as homo thugs who dressed in extra large clothing and who wore gym shorts over their boxers and then extra large jeans which sagged over their shorts. But this was not the case; he simply had on clothes which were layered one on top of the other. I knew that Chicago winters were brutal, but what he had on was over kill. And now that explained the odor, it was one of sweaty clothing which has dried and then been re-soiled with more sweat.

After he had removed the shirts, he started removing his paints. Under his jeans he had on a pair of what looked like either sweat pants of fleece pants in the dark. Under that he work three quarter shorts and under that a pair of boxers which looked like they were blue or black.

Under all the clothing he was actually thinner than me. All this time I had been thinking he had gained weight, but in reality he was really thin, almost too thin in my opinion.

For some reason the way his body looked freaked me out and I realized I wasn't feeling the sex anymore. He lay on the bed next to me and started kissing me. I tried mimicking what he was doing, but I couldn't do it, I was turned totally off. He didn't notice the change in my mood thought because by now he was all into it and I could feel that he had a slight erection on my leg as he was leaning over and kissing on my chest.

I wasn't sure how I was going to end this evening, but I knew that it was not going to end with us having sex. I was done. I started pushing him away but he took it for play resistance that occurs during sex and became more aggressive. I was lying in my stomach and he was kissing my back and moving lower. He had reached my waist and I started to get a little excited and was thinking it couldn't hurt for him to give me hand job, it didn't mean that we had to have sex for that to happen.

He moved past kissing my waist and started spreading my cheek and licking me on my ass which felt great. But my mind would not allow me to relax enough to really enjoy it. I was done. I reached behind me and moved his head away but he thought I was playing and grabbed both of my wrists and darted his tongue between my cheeks. I felt nothing and even started getting a little worried and fearful that I wouldn't be able to get him off of me. I finally pulled my hands free and got them under me for enough leverage so that I could roll over and simultaneously get him off of me.

"What's the matter?" he asked, his voice was full since he was fully turned on by now.

"I'm not in the mood anymore," I said. "I don't feel well."

Before I could get the word well out of my mouth, I felt a warm and stick liquid substance on the inner part of my thigh and I could hear him grunting in the dark. I couldn't believe it; he had gotten worked up enough to prematurely ejaculate. I wasn't even hard yet.

I bounded out of the bed and turned on the light, but he bolted from the room at the same time that I had cut on the light. The substance on my legs looked like coagulated pee. It was thick like semen but the yellow color of urine or even mucus. I felt my stomach coming into my mouth and I wanted to simply hop into a scalding hot bath. It was not only on my leg but on my sheets as well.

When he came out of the bathroom he started putting on his clothes and didn't even once make eye contact with me. He and I both knew that he was ill, but with what I didn't know. I needed a change and I needed to save myself from where I was eventually going to end up.

28

I knew I was done when I got emailed about a threesome. I declined, and then they said they had heard about me from other guys on the site who said I was good to go. Even after they told me if I ever changed my mind I should give them a call, I declined and I was grateful for the strength to do so. I deleted their number and every other number I had from Adam 4 Steve, Black Gay Convo, Thugs for Love, Sex Hunt and all the other sites.

One by one I erased their numbers from my phone, the Jay's, Tony's, Reggie's, Mike's, Marcus's, James's, Jamal's and so on the list went. I finally began to start my recovery cycle, even after I was off of the sites when I would get text messages from anyone; I began getting comfortable with the phrase, 'not interested'.

I felt like even though I needed and wanted love in my life I never understood the real meaning of love. I ended up living with an addiction and falling too easily for any man who would whisper in my ear as he was pounding me that he liked me.

I started regaining control and caring for my body. There were physical things after the first STD that was starting to happen to my body which I had been ignoring all along.

About a month before my last encounter I had noticed in the shower that there were small pimples which were coming up in and on my bottom and even directly around the anus. The first time I noticed it, I thought it was some kind of rash because I had changed the soap and perfume that I typically wore. So I simply changed back to what I normally used and for awhile, I didn't worry about it. But then one morning there were so many of them that I couldn't ignore it any longer.

I put in my physical symptoms on the internet and did a search to see what possible reasons were for the outbreak. The definition that kept returning to me on the computer was for a condition called Genital Warts.

A highly contagious sexually transmitted disease caused by some sub-types of human papillomavirus (HPV). It is spread through direct skin-to-skin contact during oral, genital, or anal sex with an infected partner.

I didn't even know how to react other than to tell myself that it had to be something else.

I eventually found myself at the nurse's office on campus that same week. Needless to say, I was embarrassed and ashamed but I knew that if I were to make not only a full mental recovery from my life, I need a physical one as well.

"So what brings you here?" she asked.

"Well I have something on my back," I said, not wanting to get too specific while still in the reception area.

"So let's see what you talking about?" she said, instructing me to turn around and she started standing up behind her desk to look over at my back.

"Oh, it's not quite my back," I whispered, taking a quick glance around the waiting room to make sure no one could hear me.

"Oh, ok, I'm sorry," she said. "Let's get you into a room."

Once I was in the room alone, I was determined never to be in this position again. I felt alone and at fault for everything that I was going through right at that moment. When the nurse entered I had already undressed and had put on the gown. She told me to lie down and show her exactly what I was referring to in the waiting room.

"It's right here," I said, bending over and spreading my cheeks apart so she could see.

"Oh I see sort of like a cauliflower color, it's a wart I believe," she said, sinking my hopes for anything other than that diagnosis.

"When did you first notice it?"

"I noticed it about two days ago when I began itching a lot," I lied.

"Ok well I'm going to quickly type this in just in case I won't be here next week so if you come in again the next nurse will know what treatment to give you," she replied.

"Tunde, I will be asking a few questions right before your treatment today," she announced.

"Ok I'm ready," I answered.

"So do you have sex with women, men or both?" she started off.

"Umm men," I answered.

"Do you have unprotected sex? Or protected sex with condoms?"

"I definitely use condoms for protected sex," I said defensively.

"That's great and how many partners do you think you have had in the past month?"

"I'm not sure maybe two or three," I replied.

"Do you think maybe more than that or you don't feel comfortable answering that question?"

"Umm three," I said again.

"So did you know that genital warts are passed on mostly from skin to skin contact?"

"No, I did not know that but I always use condoms though," I emphasized not wanting to be judged.

"Well that's great however sometimes people tend to say they allow their partners to put in the tip of their private part in them and remove it prior to ejaculation, which can be a possible way of how genital parts are passed," she continued.

"Wow I didn't know that," I said meekly.

"Yes and sometimes people say it feels good and want to keep the mood going without a condom and by mistake the other person releases in them," she added.

"Well it's not the case with me I can tell you," I said.

"When was the last time you had sex?" she asked again.

"I'm not sure maybe last month, yesterday I don't know," I answered frustrated.

"Well we can stop if the questions are getting uncomfortable"

"Yes I prefer we stop please."

Once that interview was over the other nurse came in to begin the actual treatment. First she reiterated about the warts and how they were contracted. Then she explained that it could spread so I had to stop having sex.

The good news after she had finished with the first treatment was that it would start to reduce the warts in size. But the bad news and worst part of it was that she could only take care of the warts around the exterior of my anus that were visible. For the one which they could see which were located in my anus, they would need to refer me to the larger main hospital located off campus. It would require them to complete a colorectal exam on me to see exactly how far inward the warts were located.

Leaving the clinic that day, I knew I had hit rock bottom with my addiction.

In the next few weeks it was in my own decision to disassociate with everything and everyone. I wasn't even taking Sammy and John's phone calls. I was ready to heal and be better. I knew that I could do better; I just wasn't sure where I needed to start. I didn't make a follow up appointment with the doctor until another month or so.

I just wanted to stay in bed, with the lights off to think. So I felt I needed time to myself in order to start to heal.

The follow up appointment was just a formality to confirm that the medication and treatment had worked. There was nothing else and I hadn't seen any more warts come up on my body. I was starting with a clean slate, again. Except this time I was determined to really respect and appreciate that second chance clean slate.

My first step after I had deleted all of my online accounts in the various chat rooms was to find an alternate activity that could bring me a job. The act of completing that task of deleting all my accounts alone took the better part of a day, because some of the sites seemed to make it harder to close out your membership than it was to join. I resisted the urge to check my inboxes one last time. That little voice in my head that would say, 'hey you never know, Mr. Right might have emailed you this time around', needed to be ignored. I needed to discover the Mr. Right in me first before I went searching externally.

I still participated in GLBT events in the community and went to clubs, but I made sure and never brought anyone home and absolutely without a doubt no sex. I began noticing a pattern that I had ignored before, though it had always been there. Live, the men would behave the same way that they did online, it was a ritual of sorts. Eye contact and flirtation, empty compliments about how good someone looked, exchange numbers, call the same night, talk for a few hours and hit the bedroom the next day. They were lucky if they made it to the end of the week and were now referring to each other as 'boyfriend'. Otherwise the ritual repeated itself the following week in the club.

Instead I found other things to do with my time. I started going to the center regularly and participating in some of the classes. I even offered to teach a dance class when one of the regular instructors had left. There was still drama about who had slept with who and who was trying to flirt with who now, but I didn't have to be involved with that, I left it for the ones who hadn't been where I had been and seen or experienced the things I had seen.

I started hanging out with Sammy and John again. I realized they had been trying to encourage and steer me in the right direction all along. Even Sammy, who still loved his married men, was pleased to know I had ended my long term relationship with the internet.

I had dodged the HIV/AIDS bullet twice and I was determined not to have to be that target again. I valued my life and more importantly I was starting to value the lives of others who I had put in jeopardy with my carelessness. I had wanted to email an apology to the one guy that had originally contacted me to tell me I had an STD, but when I tried, I found that he had blocked me from being able to contact him further. I didn't blame him, I had been blind to the obvious and I had learned a hard lesson.

29

My online life took on a life of its own. I met so many, some of whom had similar stories to mine, people who had given up on their lives. I came across a poem on the internet one time that has always stuck in my head.

I have a friend with benefits,
Whom off and on I see.
While I use him to get my kicks,
He also uses me.
He's not my boyfriend, just a friend
With whom I have some sex.
Too young to love, we play the game
And wonder what comes next.
We try out stuff from porno sites,
Watching what we do
As though we were on film, and someone
Else was watching, too.
Yet somehow, somewhere even we
Still know we yearn for love,
And wait like withered stalks to feel
That wind within us move.

Anonymous

Through it all deep down I was really simply searching for love but failed each time to make it work. I had given up and the best way I had found to deal with my pain was to live life by riding the back of someone else. It ended up being a horrible way for me to exist and I knew it.

If the world was my stage and I played my part, I played multiple roles; I was the whore, lost soul, sucker for love and the addict. I learned that men search for fairy tales in relationships just like women and will never admit to wanting that treasure at the end of the rainbow. It is almost like I didn't have a guide to tell me to slow down, so I headed full speed into my own near destruction. I did find love though, when I was least paying attention. It was right in me all along, more so than I found in my friends and family.

It took me awhile to realize that my body was my temple and it needed only one dweller. I was sure that the right person would come when I least expected it but I definitely wouldn't let him take me for a ride. I was determined to be in control and to do without sex in the beginning of any relationship till it was the right time. I learned the hard way that sex didn't define a relationship for me.

I don't live with regrets about what happened to me but I learned that I am worth much more than what I had originally valued myself. Today I never date someone who tells me he is too busy to communicate with me, that behavior serves as a beaming red light of warning. What I took from my experiences is what some refer to as a curse but what I call my gift that is still within me.. I will continue to take control of my life, I now feel as though I have been reborn and

I'm a new being without needing anyone's consent. Only I know how it feels to be damaged and reconstructed to be able to let go of an addiction and come to my full senses once again.

ACKNOWLEDGMENTS

I want to thank God first of all because only he knows the reason why I have chosen this path to share the stories of others through writing. I want to thank Aruelafal Atambi for being a true friend all these years and for giving me such a great advice that, "If I plan to go far sometimes I would have to plan to go alone". I want to thank my lovely sister Oyinda, I love you, thanks for being by me whenever I felt alone on my path to follow my dreams. Thank you mom for showing support no matter what path I chose in life and thank you for being a friend and a mother, love you. I want thank the rest of my family for showing support over the years and getting me back on track during my years of doubt. Thank you to John Adewoye and Kenny Dee for being inspirations and providing a home away from home with love and support.

Thank you Cody, Demint, Dion, Halina, Mrs. Hattie, Daniel, Marc and Nicole for making me stay focused on my goals rather than partying and wasting away my time. Thank you to my publisher Michelle Dixon because you made it happen by taking me into the Lalibra Books family to be able to tell a great story. Lastly thanks to all who have given me a story to share in this novel and together we can put an end to giving up and letting go of addictions to be reborn.

ABOUT THE AUTHOR

Biodun Abudu was born in Rhode Island, but comes from a Nigerian background. When he is not writing, he works as a model, choreographer, drag performer, actor and fashion designer. In 2011, he graduated with an. A.S. degree in Fashion Design and a B.A. in Merchandising Management with an emphasis on Fashion Merchandising. He currently resides in the Chicago metropolitan area.

Made in the USA
Charleston, SC
29 October 2011